THE ALFRED HITCHCOCK MOVIE QUIZ BOOK

A THE ALFRED HITCHCOCK
MOVIE QUIZ BOOK

Bryan Brown

A Perigee Book

Perigee Books
are published by
The Putnam Publishing Group
200 Madison Avenue
New York, NY 10016

*All photographs courtesy of Universal Pictures and
Jerry Ohlinger's Movie Material Store.*

Library of Congress Cataloging-in-Publication Data

Brown, Bryan, date.
  The Alfred Hitchcock movie quiz book.

  1. Hitchcock, Alfred, 1899–   —Miscellanea.
2. Moving-pictures—Miscellanea.   I. Title.
PN1998.A3H533   1986   791.43′0233′0924   85-29876
ISBN 0-399-51221-7

Printed in the United States of America
1 2 3 4 5 6 7 8 9 10

ACKNOWLEDGMENTS

Many thanks go to Sherry Robb, Bart Andrews and Jim Pinkston, the author's agents. Bob Torsello, Dale Kent (and Kent Enterprises) and Freddie Wensig deserve extreme thanks for their invaluable editorial help, their VCR (a wonderful invention, that) and Parmesan-cheesed meals. Thanks also to Mercedes Montgomery-John and Mark Winders for their southern New Jersey hospitality; to Jerry Ohlinger's Movie Material Store, one of the rare non–anally retentive movie-still suppliers in New York; and to Vincent Virga who quelled the author's anxiety attack over photographs. Finally, and most vociferously, thanks to Joe Pheifer, fellow Kinks lover, who actually wanted to edit the book, and to Susan Bailey, a good soul who deserves credit (or blame) for the whole idea. Go in peace . . .

A word about books: This book would not have been nearly as good without the benefit of many others. François Truffaut's *Hitchcock* was probably the most important in terms of sparking fascination in an impressionable adolescent mind. It has recently been reissued by Simon and Schuster/Touchstone with lots of nifty new pictures. Also invaluable are Donald Spoto's two books, *The Art of Alfred Hitchcock* (Dolphin/Doubleday) and *The Dark Side of Genius* (Little, Brown, cloth; Ballantine, paper). Robin Wood's *Hitchcock's Films* has been out of print for years but is worth picking up in used-book shops or from a library. Other in-print books that are entertaining and informative in a significant sense are *The Strange Case of Alfred Hitchcock* by Raymond Durgnat (MIT Press), *Hitchcock: The Murderous Gaze* by William Rothman (Harvard University Press) and the original Hitchcock book, *Hitchcock: The First Forty-Four Films* by Eric Rohmer and Claude Chabrol (Frederick Ungar Publishing).

To Kathy, who kept me alive

Contents

Introduction
Of the Purposes and Idiosyncrasies of This Book

*I don't bother about plot, or all that kind of thing. . . . That's—
what shall I call it—that's a necessary evil.*—Alfred Hitchcock

THIS book was born of a small obsession, nestled and kept warmed and watered in a slightly fearful, more-than-slightly resentful adolescent bosom. This obsession comes to you today in its present unwieldy (but attractively packaged) form, not as a film journal exegesis, or a documentary, or an academic lecture, or truck bomb or any other sort of sociopathology, but as . . . a quiz book: a book of quizzes about the films of Alfred Hitchcock, who for fifty-odd years made some of the most fearful, resentful, wickedly funny movies the world is likely to see. This much about Hitchcock the reader must grant us. Whether or not you are willing to admit greatness for this strange man is another matter, but we are prepared to submit evidence of a limited, human sort of greatness for him and his movies. What we see in Hitchcock's work is the unique artistic vision of a misanthropic film genius.

I am of the generation that knew Alfred Hitchcock first as a vaguely frightening image on television, then as a maker of the thrilling kind of entertainments that one would boldly see and brag about with peers, qualifying one as being up on the latest rage and unafraid of the world beyond school. *Psycho* and *The Birds* were almost rites of initiation. Only later, through the scouring of books, repeated viewings and a clearer view of adult sadness, did his movies reveal things about a man's mind, and a man's life, that were far more complicated than (although they certainly did not exclude) scaring people out of their silly minds.

Doubtless you are wondering what all this highfalutin nonsense has to do with the quiz book you are holding. And you may be skeptical about the nutritional value of this enterprise, remembering such fiascoes as *The Russian Literature Quiz Book* ("Raskolnikov killed the landlady with (a) the cleat of his hiking boot, (b) conveniently placed fishing tackle. . . ."). We will say this: We have tried to steer a center course between the profound and the trivial, since the former is often hard to ask short-answer questions about and the latter is often boring. What we were most fascinated about in looking at Hitchcock movies were their structure, character motivations and points of those much-forgotten (even by Hitchcock) plots. Also, we were fascinated by who made Rebecca's underwear.

Most of the quizzes in this volume deal with a specific movie. The "Beginnings" quiz covers all of the silents (except *The Lodger*) and most of the pre–*Man Who Knew Too Much* movies. In addition, there are other exercises, which we will call "Theme Quizzes," for lack of a better term, that presume a familiarity on the part of the reader for the whole of Hitchcock's career. The questions in each quiz add up to a convenient 100 points; the Extra Credit questions give the irritatingly knowledgeable a chance to flaunt their knowledge in all things Hitchcock. As the Good Book says, to he who has will more be given. . . . The questions themselves are mostly short-answer, with the odd multiple choice, match-up and the very odd True and False. Also, there is the Word Association tactic, in which the idea is to say the first thing that comes into the mind (as long as it's right, of course). This type of questioning you'll remember from reform school.

All said, we cannot possibly hope to duplicate the experience of seeing the movies themselves. So many images come to mind—the key in Alicia Huberman's hand, the strangling of Miriam Haines, Charlie Newton coming down the stairs with the murdered woman's ring—that we can't do justice to. And we're not even trying to step on the film scholar's turf. We're just out for a little fun, okay? So go ahead and buy the bloody book and enjoy it. Of course we recommend repeated viewings of most of these films, especially, for example, *Strangers on a Train*, as they will enable one to do well in these quizzes without cheating. We have tried to be accurate without obsessing about it: Hitchcock himself was always going on about the "plausibles"—he was only plausible when he felt like it. Just relax and use your head—but not too much. And in case of the onset of trauma, just insert a copy of the book between the tongue and the roof of the mouth and introduce a large brandy to the traumatized area.

ABOUT SCORING

The Secretary has applied the following scale of judgment to the hypothetical quiz-taker's score on each or all of the quizzes in this book, when taken in the United States, its territories and possessions (excluding Bergen County, New Jersey).

Above 100: Know-it-all

90–100: Expert

70–88: Highly perceptive

50–68: Normal

30–48: Dilettante

10–28: Legally blind

Under 10: Executive material

Beginnings (1925–1933)

AFTER a brief career in the British film industry designing titles and sets, and eventually serving as assistant director under Graham Cutts for several projects, Hitchcock got his own project from Michael Balcon of Gainsborough Pictures. *The Pleasure Garden* (1925) would be the first finished movie directed by Alfred Hitchcock. This little quiz deals with the majority of pictures made for Balcon at Gainsborough and for John Maxwell at British International Pictures—the exceptions are *The Lodger, Blackmail* and *Murder!*, which are of especial interest and follow hard upon this chapter's heels. For all but the most obsessive of Hitchcock scholars, these films must appear medieval. Indeed, they are treated as historical relics, rather than movies—if they get shown at all, it is in museums. All of them are incredibly dated, of course, and the dialogue of the early talkies is all but indecipherable (we have seen *Number Seventeen* twice and *still* don't know what happened), but most of them have something to recommend them, and some of them are quite good. Most of these pictures were assignments from Maxwell and would be shot with an increasing lack of interest by Hitchcock. While Hitchcock made some striking pictures during this period, it was not until he got out of his BIP contract and returned to work for Balcon at Gaumont-British that he came into his own with *The Man Who Knew Too Much*.

Part I

This exercise will require the participant to match each of the following synopses to the appropriate title. (All questions worth 5 points.)
The films we will deal with are:

The Pleasure Garden (1925)   *The Manxman* (1929)

The Mountain Eagle (1926)   *Juno and the Paycock* (1930)

Downhill (1927)   *The Skin Game* (1931)

Easy Virtue (1927)   *Rich and Strange* (1932)

The Ring (1927)   *Number Seventeen* (1932)

The Farmer's Wife (1928)   *Waltzes From Vienna* (1933)

Champagne (1928)

1. Larita Filton finds her hypocritical in-laws unforgiving of a somewhat checkered past, and her husband is a similar sap for propriety.

2. Fred and Emily Hill, relieved from the dullness of the work week by a generous departed uncle, travel to distant climes, separate for respective flings, survive a shipwreck, eat a cat and end up together after all.

3. An Irish family survives the civil war.

4. An amenable fellow takes the rap for a school chum's illegitimate child, getting drubbed out of school, disinherited and exiled to a life of dispirited traveling as a result. Eventually the offending party owns up and life resumes.

5. Patsy loves Hugh but Hugh loves Jill so Patsy marries Levett, who drowns his mistress, tries to kill Patsy, and is in turn shot by the doctor, leaving a delirious Hugh, jilted by Jill, to marry Patsy.

6. "One Round" Jack is in love with Nelly, who in turn dallies with Bob, another boxer, before making up her mind.

7. Pete the fisherman marries Kate, but Philip the lawyer has gotten there first, and a baby of uncertain origin arrives. Philip

in the meantime has chosen a career over romantic intrigue, but when Kate leaves Pete, attempts suicide, and is hauled before Judge Philip, he realizes the jig is up.

8. Betty's father flinches at her flapper-ed flippancy and claims the family fortune is fallen. It isn't, really. After some hard work and some growing up—during which she sells the family product at a cabaret—all is forgiven and everyone is happy.

9. Pettigrew lusts for Beatrice, who takes refuge with Fear O'God in the mountains of Kentucky.

10. Squire Sweetland courts three unlikely wife prospects, until realizing the best one—the cute Minta—is right under his nose.

11. The life of Johann Strauss, wigged composer.

12. Bucolic Hillcrist and nouveau riche Hornblower slug it out on adjoining pieces of land.

13. Designed as a parody of thrillers, in which a young man and a bum come across a dead body in an abandoned house, which eventually comes to life and has a beautiful daughter to boot. Young man and beautiful girl are handcuffed to rickety railing, which collapses. Sympathetic characters have a race with baddies in which several models get smashed up.

Part II

14. For which of these films is there no existing print?

15. What is the Pleasure Garden?

16. In which film is the much-sought-after girl presented with a serpent-shaped bracelet?

17. Which film is based on a Sean O'Casey play?

18. Which is based on a Noël Coward play?

19. Which is based on a John Galsworthy play?

20. What was Hitchcock's own least favorite film, according to Hitchcock in the Truffaut book?

Extra Credit

21. Which film was Hitchcock's last silent?

22. What was the name of the British music/comedy film for which Hitchcock contributed "sketches and other interpolated items"?

23. What was the name of the one film Hitchcock produced during this period, handing the direction to Benn Levy?

THE LODGER (1926)

Hitchcock's third film was, as the director said, the first "Hitchcock film"—the first thriller, the first Wrong Man picture, etc. It also made his reputation (for a time), but thanks to the imposition of office politics was almost not shown. John Russell Taylor's and Donald Spoto's biographies tell a fascinating story of the jealousy and resentment that dogged Hitchcock throughout his early days as the boy wonder at Gainsborough Pictures. (All questions worth 10 points or as indicated.)

1. What have the papers dubbed the serial killer?

2. What does our killer look for in a victim?

3. Apparently the killer only works one day a week. Which is it?

4. What is Daisy Bunting's profession?

5. What is the name of the newspaper that sees to the whipping up of public hysteria?

6. What is the Lodger's mission? Who has sworn him to it? (Five points each.)

7. What was the scene of the murder the Lodger means to avenge?

8. Joe Betts, the jealous puppy-dog suitor (and cop), and Mom and Pop Bunting begin to suspect the Lodger of being the murderer

and worry about their Daisy's safety. What gift of the Lodger's to Daisy does her father make her return?

9. Who besides the Lodger gets handcuffed in this film?

10. The Lodger, like the killer, carries a mysterious black bag. What is in the Lodger's?

Extra Credit

11. How much time passes between the beginning of the film and the capture of the murderer?

12. What was the ending Hitchcock claimed the studio would not let him use?

13. Who was the film writer/critic that Michael Balcon brought in to help save the film, and what was his contribution?

BLACKMAIL (1929)

Alfred Hitchcock's first talking picture also marked the beginning of the director's long association with Charles Bennett, who wrote the stage play *Blackmail* is based on. It is an effective little rumination—typically Hitchcock—on the inseparability and confusion of guilt and innocence, yet full of those inexplicable pauses that plagued the early talkies, the chief beneficiary of which is John Longden, who gets to glower dramatically for minutes on end at the blackmailer before delivering each line. *Blackmail* also features Hitchcock's first extended cameo. (All questions worth 10 points or as indicated.)

1. What are Alice and Frank arguing about at the restaurant?

2. Do the artist and Alice meet there by accident?

3. What painting of the artist's does Alice take exception to?

4. What evidence does Frank remove from the scene of the crime?

5. What evidence does the blackmailer present to the happy couple of his knowledge of the crime?

6. What unsavory business have we already witnessed the blackmailer in before he comes into Mr. White's store?

7. Alice wanders around after the murder, and, like characters in many Hitchcock films, guiltily associates her surroundings with her crime. What does she see in the neon Gordon's Gin sign in Piccadilly?

8. Who identifies the blackmailer—in the opinion of the police, anyway—as the murderer?

9. Where do the police catch up with the blackmailer?

10. What finally prevents Alice from giving her confession?

Extra Credit

11. What day does the story begin on?

12. What is the blackmailer's name?

13. Who did the dialogue for Anny Ondra, and why? (Five points each.)

MURDER! (1930)

A sort of Wrong Woman tale, *Murder!* centers on Sir John Menier, an actor/playwright who, when sitting on a jury in a murder trial, allows himself to be bulldozed by the other impatient jurors into delivering a guilty verdict against his instincts—and who feels so remorseful afterward that he sets out to find the murderer himself. A very interesting film concerned with the theater—the actor's melodramatic confusion of art and reality and all that jazz ("This is *life*," says Sir John, surprised at its unexpected intrusion)—and bold in its depiction of sexual ambiguity. It contains a Hamlet-like play within a play designed to entrap the suspected murderer, the only documented case of false teeth in a Hitchcock film, and an inner monologue that pops up in Herbert Marshall's head while he is shaving and listening to the radio, which, because of a lack of postdubbing, had to be executed with a tape recording of his voice and a thirty-piece orchestra on the set. *Murder!* is also notable for the presence of improvised dialogue; this accounts for the occasional impression of Quaalude abuse some of the scenes give. (All questions worth 10 points or as indicated.)

1. What is the professional connection between the victim, the murderer and the falsely accused woman? What is the personal connection between the last two? (Five points each.)

2. Diana Baring, convicted for Edna Druce's murder, is found in a daze at the scene. What is her defense? Why was Edna killed? (Five points each.)

3. What disguise did Handell Fane don while wandering around the night of the murder? Why didn't Diana hear him come in? (Five points each.)

4. Sir John is obviously feeling guilty and at the same time falling in love with Diana. Where had he previously met her? And what does he find in Diana's room that would seem to indicate that she also has more than a passing interest in him? (Five points each.)

5. What is Sir John's first strong inkling that someone else was at the scene of the crime?

6. What is the first piece of evidence that ties Handell Fane to the scene of the crime? What other significant clue do Markham and Sir John come across in Fane's abandoned dressing room? (Five points each.)

7. How many people initially vote to acquit Diana during the jury's deliberation?

8. What inducements does Sir John give Ted and Dulcie Markham to join his investigation? (Five points each.)

9. Sir John's play about "the inner history of the Baring case" is, as he says, his version of Hamlet's little play *The Mousetrap*. What, as Markham asks, is the cheese? And, as Fane gets more

and more leery about Sir John's reasons for "auditioning" him, what about the Baring play finally cinches his suspicions that Sir John is wise to him? (Five points each.)

10. How does Handell Fane's former profession (a) aid him in performance of the murder, and (b) aid him in atoning for his guilt at Diana's conviction and keep him out of Sir John's hands? (Five points each.)

Extra Credit

11. What time did the murder take place?

12. What pieces of music are played under the credits and while Sir John is shaving? (Five points each.)

13. What is the landlady's name?

14. What was the name of the German-language version of *Murder!*?

The Major British Years
(1934–1939)

By the end of 1933 Hitchcock was at the end of his tether, disheartened by a long, frustrating association with British International Pictures and directing with extreme and hostile disinterest *Waltzes From Vienna*, a musical that he would later describe as his worst picture. His reputation, which had soared with *The Lodger* some six years before, had fallen steadily (with the exception of two or three points) during his years at BIP, partly because of the lack of enthusiasm he felt for many of the assignments handed to him by John Maxwell, his producer. At this point Michael Balcon came to the rescue by buying a film idea of Hitchcock's and Charles Bennett's and then signing both of them to a five-picture contract at Gaumont-British Pictures, where Balcon was producing. This film became the first *The Man Who Knew Too Much*, a huge boon to Hitchcock's career. The remainder of his films with Balcon would cinch his reputation as a superior director of suspense stories and establish him as a worldwide presence in the cinema. There are not a few critics who would claim that this period is Hitchcock's most creative; it is an arguable proposition. In any case this period did produce two of the most popular Hitchcocks of all time, *The 39 Steps* and *The Lady Vanishes*, films that still appear in revival houses and on college campuses with astounding frequency.

THE MAN WHO KNEW TOO MUCH (1934 and 1956)

It is now that we contribute our two cents, in a rather more whimsical fashion than usual, to the ongoing debate concerning the relative merits of the two versions of this film. Having no critical reputation at stake, we can allow a fondness for both versions. The British version is much funnier, but on balance not as rich as the American. On the other hand, there are all those crowd-pleasing Hollywoodisms in the '56 version—an impossibly "cute" kid that you want to strangle and the repetition of . . . *that song*. The first *Man* was definitely a watershed in Hitchcock's career, reestablishing his flagging critical reputation and a crucial link with producer Michael Balcon. The story in both versions is basically the same: a couple on holiday with their young child is accidentally privy to a dying spy's story that an assassination is planned in London. The couple's child is kidnapped to ensure their silence and they travel to London, ignoring the authorities' demand for information. The mother ends up at Royal Albert Hall, where the assassination is planned to take place, emits an auspicious scream when the clash of the cymbals is meant to cover the sound of gunfire, and in effect spoils the murder. Both versions end happily, with family reunited and conspirators (at least most of them) expired. (All questions worth 4 points.)

Part I

Supply the elements that differ in the two versions.

1934   1956

1. The mother's present/past career/avocation.
2. Locale of opening.
3. Couple's hometown.
4. Name of child.
5. Location of the spiritual interlude.
6. Manner of Louis Bernard's death.
7. Manner of the assassin's death.
8. Manner of the kidnapper's death.

9. Why do the mothers in each version end up going to Albert Hall?

10. The assassins are played the piece of music so that they might recognize the moment when they are to shoot. Which of the assassins gets a look at a musical score?

11. What major character in the 1934 version has no counterpart in the 1956 film?

12. Which conspiratory role in 1956 is comparatively small in 1934?

Part II

A short identification quiz based totally on the 1956 version.

13. FBI.

14. Snails.

15. "We'll Love Again."

16. Adversity.

Part III

Assorted questions.

17. 1934: What sends Bob and Clive to the dentist's?

18. 1934: Where do we first see the symbol for the Tabernacle of the Sun?

19. 1956: In general, what has paid for the McKennas' trip abroad? (Just for the sake of argument, the especially observant may be awarded 2 points for each specific item.)

20. 1956: What does Louis Bernard tell Jo is his profession?

21. 1956: The McKennas, in finding Ambrose Chapel, discover the Draytons in atypically ecclesiastical pursuits. What exactly is Mrs. Drayton doing when she spots them?

22. 1956: Of what office and nationality is the proposed assassination target?

23. 1956: Who sponsors the assassination?

24. 1956: What longtime Hitchcock collaborator appears in the Albert Hall scene?

25. What piece of music is used for both Albert Hall sequences?

Extra Credit

26. 1956: Why does Louis Bernard apparently latch onto the McKennas?

27. 1956: From whom did Hitchcock purchase the rights to the remake?

28. 1934: What problem did the British Board of Film Censors have with the ending of this film?

29. 1934: What information on the shaving-brush note turns out to be wrong?

THE 39 STEPS (1935)

Contains the first "Hitchcock blonde," Madeleine Carroll, the first extended use of handcuffs, perhaps the first conscious "MacGuffin," the first "picaresque" (if you'll forgive us) Wrong Man chase, the first suavely respectable villain, the superlative Mr. Memory and the insouciant Robert Donat (with, as Raymond Durgnat says, his "anyone for tennis?" look). Adapted by Charles Bennett, with dialogue by Ian Hay, from a novel by John Buchan, a writer much admired by Hitchcock and by Graham Greene, *The 39 Steps* is one of the most popular Hitchcocks ever. (All questions worth 10 points.)

1. What question does Richard Hannay have for Mr. Memory the first time he takes in the show?

2. In general, whom does Annabella Smith, our international spy, usually work for?

3. From which hand is Professor Jordan missing the digit of his little finger?

4. How does the farmer's loveless piety—an unfortunate cross indeed for his poor wife—turn out to be a very *good* thing for Richard Hannay?

5. Pamela, our reluctant heroine, rats on Hannay twice before she comes to believe his story. Where were those two occasions?

6. What finally changes Pamela's mind about Hannay?

7. What is the significance of the tune that has been stuck in Hannay's head throughout the progression of the story?

8. The film begins and ends in the London Palladium—what sends Hannay back there?

9. How many facts does Mr. Memory memorize each day? What are these 39 steps, anyway? (Five points each.)

10. Finally, what is the secret that has caused all the commotion?

Extra Credit

11. What is Alt-na Shellach?

12. What is Crazy Month?

13. What very valuable member of the Hitchcock production team began her association with the director as his secretary on this picture?

14. What little practical joke of questionable taste did the director play on his leading man and lady the first day of shooting?

SECRET AGENT (1936)

Some longtime Hitchcock themes are explored in this film—the confusion between love and duty, and duty and personal morality; the ugliness that can result when the bored wish too strongly for excitement, and then get it. Elsa grins and makes her finger into a gun when Ashenden asks her what she wants out of the assignment. Of course when the shoot-'em-up starts, she gets sore at him, as if it were his idea. Doesn't it figure? (All questions worth 10 points or as indicated.)

1. In what year does the story take place?

2. The newly christened Richard Ashenden—what were his former name and profession? (Five points each.)

3. Why has Ashenden's former life been so unceremoniously killed off?

4. What is the name of Ashenden's superior?

5. Where is the German agent headed, and why? (Five points each.)

6. What is the General's specific purpose on this mission?

7. What makes our spies suspect poor Mr. Caypor of being the German agent?

8. Mr. Caypor's dog appears to be telepathic, reacting in alarm when his master is threatened. What two scenes make the animal hysterical with worry? (Five points each.)

9. Where are the German spies' headquarters?

10. How do our heroes finally come up with the real agent's name?

Extra Credit

11. Being a spy picture and all, *Secret Agent* features an appropriate number of secret messages and coded notes, the proper translations thoughtfully provided for the uninitiated. We counted nine notes in all, seven of them passed back and forth between our heroes and their accomplices. The other two notes were initiated by the enemy—where did they appear and what did they say? (Five points for each note.)

12. What does the final message of the film say?

13. Why does Elsa demand that Ashenden refrain from killing Marvin?

14. What was Peter Lorre's biggest problem during filming?

SABOTAGE (1936)

Loosely adapted from Conrad's *The Secret Agent*, *Sabotage* continues Hitchcock's streak of vaguely German villains. "London must not laugh at us," they decree in *Sabotage*, and execute a series of public demonstrations of their unamusement. Containing one of the most truly suspenseful scenes in the Hitchcock catalogue—the late delivery of the bomb by Stevie—and the first domestic murder—of Mr. Verloc by his missus—this film marks the end of an era for Hitchcock as it would be the last he would ever do for Michael Balcon. (All questions worth 10 points or as indicated.)

1. The story takes place in four days, Wednesday through Saturday. What is so special about Saturday that it should rate a public demonstration of irritability from our saboteurs?

2. How does Verloc effect his bit of sabotage at the beginning of the film?

3. Why won't Verloc's superior pay him for his work?

4. What is the name of Verloc's movie house?

5. Our friendly greengrocer/super cop next door to the cinema is watching old Verloc. What blows his cover?

6. Bird imagery: When Verloc goes to the pet shop to pick up his bomb, there is a woman trying to return a canary. What is her complaint?

7. What does Verloc bring the bomb home in?

8. What does the note say that Verloc gets from his saboteur pals on the big day?

9. What is poor Stevie's destination when he is given the can of film and its accompanying gift-wrapped bomb? Why is he almost prevented from getting on the bus by the bus driver? (Five points each.)

10. What saves poor Mrs. Verloc from getting arrested for stabbing Mr. Verloc?

Extra Credit

11. What is the name of the film Stevie is carrying?

12. What is the name of the cartoon that Mrs. Verloc takes in after learning of Stevie's death?

YOUNG AND INNOCENT (1937)

A little domestic quarrel ends with an expired wife, a man wrongly accused of murder and an oft-repeated Hitchcock plot development wherein a pretty young woman is pressed into reluctant service by the hero, comes to believe in her Wrong Man's innocence, and ultimately helps him clear his name, achieving romantic bliss in the bargain. This is not exactly the most intense of Hitchcock films; our hero scarcely looks worried the whole picture. The film does contain one of Hitchcock's most famous crane shots (prefiguring the key scene in *Notorious*) in which the murderer is revealed in a crowded ballroom. (All questions worth 10 points or as indicated.)

1. What are the husband and wife quarreling about at the film's opening?

2. Robert Tisdall appears to know the murdered woman. What was their connection?

3. What are the two pieces of circumstantial evidence held against Robert? (Five points each.)

4. What is the one piece of physical evidence held against Robert?

5. Why do Robert and Erica go to Tom's Hat?

6. What makes the tramp Old Will so important to our hero?

7. What is Old Will's nickname? How does Robert find him at the common shelter? (Five points each.)

8. What gift does Robert bring to the birthday party?

9. Robert is able to make two escapes during the course of the story when someone's eyesight is affected. What happens in each instance? (Five points each.)

10. What is Robert's only clue to the possible whereabouts of the murderer?

Extra Credit

11. What was the name of the common shelter?

12. What is the subject of the song the orchestra is playing when the murderer has his collapse?

13. What was the American title of this picture?

14. Optional essay: Why would it seem logical that the murder was premeditated?

THE LADY VANISHES (1938)

A very popular movie, slam-bang virtuoso entertainment, and meant to be Hitchcock's farewell to a dazzled England while the director waltzed off to Hollywood (a graceful exit vitiated, unfortunately, by that stinker *Jamaica Inn*). In addition to being highly amusing, the movie is also something of a political allegory. Just as *Foreign Correspondent* would urge American intervention into the war a couple of years later, *The Lady Vanishes* came on the heels of Neville Chamberlain's famous visit to Munich (with its accompanying sellout of Czechoslovakia) and seems to urge an end of Nazi appeasement. With its decidedly Germanic nasties and echoes of coming war, the film rouses its decent-but-complacent Britishers— who all at first deny seeing Miss Froy—into action, and gives its resident Isolationist his comeuppance. (All questions worth 10 points.)

1. What is Miss Froy's mission?

2. Who is Miss Froy's contact at the inn?

3. What is our friend Gilbert's profession?

4. What is the first attempt to render Miss Froy inoperable, or at least to put her under Dr. Hartz's care?

5. What convinces Gilbert that Iris did not hallucinate Miss Froy?

6. The Italian in Iris's compartment turns out to be a magician. What very appropriate special trick does he apparently feature in his act?

7. The bandaged patient who is brought on board the train is accompanied by a nun. What gives the nun away as not being kosher?

8. Why does the nun turn against her employer?

9. Who is the only Brit on board not to rally 'round the flag during the final shootout?

10. How does Iris herself become a vanishing lady at the end of the picture?

Extra Credit

11. What are the names of the two British cricket aficionados?

12. How did Hitchcock's preparations for the script of *The Lady Vanishes* differ from his usual obsessive involvement?

JAMAICA INN (1939)

Boy, does this one age poorly. A lame, disinterested effort, distinguished only by Charles Laughton's campy performance ("You're neither a philosopher nor a gentleman—you made sure, no survivors?"), Maureen O'Hara's cheekbones and the thug with the top hat. This quiz, like many romantic relationships, is all or nothing. (All questions worth 100 points.)

1. What is the name of Squire Pengallan's horse?

Photo Quiz I: Funny Papers

(All questions worth 10 points.)

1. What is this man doing to his brother-in-law's newspaper?
2. What is significant about the little piece of paper that he tears off?
3. Where do we find out what that piece of paper says?

4. What is this poor woman holding?

5. What is circled on this piece of paper?

6. What is this man reading?

7. Who is the author of these letters?

8. What *other* letter do these letters make reference to?

9. What is this man photographing?

10. Who will soon arrive in this room, angry at having misplaced his briefcase?

The Great Appearances Quiz

FOR most of Hitchcock's cameos he was just walking by or standing around, but in the following he is identifiable in some meaningful endeavor. Match up the appearance with the appropriate film. (All questions worth 5 points.)

1. Winding a clock
2. Holding thirteen spades
3. Riding a wheelchair
4. Walking two terriers
5. Posing at a class reunion
6. Trying to read a book, unsuccessfully
7. Losing a race with a bus door
8. Carrying a cello
9. Draining a champagne glass
10. Carrying a double bass
11. "Reduco"
12. In a cowboy hat
13. Fumbling with a camera
14. Smoking in a crowded elevator
15. In neon

a. *The Birds*
b. *Lifeboat*
c. *Young and Innocent*
d. *Psycho*
e. *Strangers on a Train*
f. *Topaz*
g. *Stage Fright*
h. *Rope*
i. *Blackmail*
j. *Spellbound*
k. *The Paradine Case*
l. *Dial M for Murder*
m. *North by Northwest*
n. *Shadow of a Doubt*
o. *The Lodger*

16. Staring at a woman who is   p. *Notorious*
    talking to herself
17. Sitting in a newsroom   q. *Rear Window*

18. For which film was an introduction substituted for a cameo?

19. What was the first cameo?

20. What was the longest cameo?

Extra Credit

21. What cameo was originally planned for *Frenzy*, then substituted with a standard standing-around appearance?

Quotes Quiz I.

Identify the film and the speaker or actor for each of the following. (All questions worth 5 points.)

1. "People don't commit murder on credit."

2. "Too late, I've put my face on."

3. "Do you know if you ripped off the fronts of houses you'd find swine?"

4. "A son is a poor substitute for a lover."

5. "They're onto you."

6. "Murder is a crime for most. . . ." "But a privilege for the few."

7. "Some people are better off dead, like your wife and my father for instance."

8. "I'm honest because with you I think it's the best way to get results."

9. "I've never caught a jewel thief before. It's very stimulating."

10. "All the information's inside Memory's head."

11. "Now I remember how nice he was. How nice we both were. Very nice."

12. "Don't confide in me, just pour me some tea."

13. "Back in your gilded cage, Melanie Daniels."

14. "What good is a hep cat with one gam missing?"

15. "She will be removed from the hospital there and operated on. Unfortunately, the operation will not be successful. Oh, I should perhaps have explained. The operation will be performed by me."

16. "I love you—I worship you—I'm used to you."

17. "Look at you and me, plunged into despair because we find out a man didn't kill his wife. We're two of the most frightening ghouls I've ever known."

18. "Oh, Forio, if you have to bite anyone, bite me."

19. "You can't fight her. No one ever got the better of her. She was beaten in the end. But it wasn't a man, it wasn't a woman—it was the sea."

20. "Women make the best psychoanalysts until they fall in love. After that they make the best patients."

Hollywood and Selznick
(1940–1947)

WITH his departure for Hollywood in March 1939, Hitchcock made a major advance in his career. The big budgets and technical superiority of Hollywood represented a quantum leap over the British film industry, and it was clear that to make the kind of movies and achieve the kind of fame he wanted Hitchcock would have to go to America. The final catalyst was his seven-year contract with David O. Selznick, producer and neurotic extraordinaire, a much-ballyhooed deal. The two men did not have the most sanguine of relationships. Selznick was increasingly obsessive about a series of other projects, not the least of which would be Jennifer Jones, and he became more and more distracted and frustrated at the director's equally stubborn willfulness. He ended up producing exactly three Hitchcock films during those seven years, selling Hitchcock's services to various studios at great profit for the balance. Artistically, those years were a mixed bag for Hitchcock—he himself might have pleaded a lack of control over projects—but at least two movies, *Shadow of a Doubt* and *Notorious*, emerge as Hitchcock masterpieces. Personally, the time was also rough for him; the fact that he was to leave his country and his family just as Hitler was getting increasingly fidgety was to cause him no little grief.

For their first project together, Selznick was dreaming up dollar signs over a Hitchcock film about the *Titanic*. The director humored Selznick, but apparently had no intention of doing such a story. He had his eye, instead, on a soon-to-be-published novel by Daphne

Du Maurier, which he would later claim was not a natural Hitchcock story—as if it had been Selznick's idea.

REBECCA (1940)

Hitchcock's first American picture, made under the omniscient eye
of David O. Selznick, was only one of three movies that the producer would keep for his own company during the stormy years of
their seven-year contract. Selznick purportedly demanded absolute
fidelity to Daphne Du Maurier's hugely popular, hyperromantic
novel. Appropriately, the film has many traditional gothic elements:
the creaky haunted house, the cranky romantic hero, the evil step-
mother figure and the storm-tossed Cinderella figure. "It's not a
Hitchcock picture," Hitchcock said, but it does hold up surprisingly
well—and does fit, with its emphasis on the oppressing dead, the
ubiquitous Rebecca, into the greater Hitchcock thematic catalogue.
(All questions worth 10 points or as indicated.)

1. What is the second Mrs. de Winter's first name?

2. What is the standard explanation of Rebecca's death, up until
   the late stages of the story? How did she really die? (Five points
   each.)

3. Who is Jack Favell, and why is he so central to the final confrontation between Rebecca and Maxim? (Five points each.)

4. What possession of Rebecca's does Mrs. de Winter break, and
   how does it send the household into an uproar? (Five points
   each.)

5. How does Mrs. Danvers spoil Mrs. de Winter's costume party?
   What is her suggested remedy for her mistress's distress immediately following? (Five points each.)

For Questions 6–8, identify the following:

6. Van Hopper.

7. Jasper.

8. The nuns of St. Mary's.

9. Who lives in the boathouse and what is his standard line about Rebecca? (Five points each.)

10. After the body is found, a reopened inquest commences, with the egregious Favell as chief accuser. A trip by all concerned to Rebecca's doctor in London ensues. What does Favell expect the doctor to say that will convict Maxim of murder? And what does the doctor say that gets Maxim off the hook? (Five points each.)

Extra Credit

11. True or false: Joan Fontaine won an Oscar for Best Actress for her role in *Rebecca*.

12. What significant element of the plot was changed to forestall intervention by the Hays office?

13. Hitchcock, in his Truffaut interview, refers to an inanimate object as "one of the three characters of the picture." To what does he refer?

FOREIGN CORRESPONDENT (1940)

How curious these impassioned World War II films seem now, with their stirring patriotic music and milk-fed sweethearts keeping assorted home fires smoldering. Hitchcock's wartime movies hold up surprisingly well, including this obvious plea for American entrance into the European conflict. "They're listening in America, Johnny," Laraine Day says to Joel McCrea, as the boy waxes on "off the cuff" and the poor technicians get laced with shrapnel. "Hello, America! Hang on to your lights! They're the only ones left in the world!" Quite often in the cinema the most inventive filmmaking coexists cheek-by-jowl with some of the silliest dialogue ("I'm in love with you and I want to marry you." "I'm in love with *you* and I want to marry *you*."—this not ten minutes after they have met). (All questions worth 10 points or as indicated.)

1. What is the name of Johnny Jones's newspaper?

2. What name does Mr. Powers give his new foreign correspondent?

3. What organization does Stephen Fisher run?

4. How many bowler hats does Johnny lose before he finally switches back to the American reporter variety?

5. What exactly is it 'that Mr. Van Meer knows that everyone wants to find out? What two countries are most intimately involved? (Five points each.)

6. How many other people know what Mr. Van Meer knows?

7. In what city is the fake Van Meer assassinated?

8. Why does the windmill turn the wrong way?

9. a. What is the name of the German at Fisher's house?
   b. What is the name of the fellow they hire to kill Jones? (Five points each.)

10. How does conventional propriety foil ffolliott's scheme for forcing Fisher's hand and getting him to expose himself?

Extra Credit

11. Walter Wanger, the producer, was constantly after Hitchcock to make the film more timely, to modify the story at every turn to reflect the current stage of the war. Hitchcock ignored him pretty much, except for one scene that was added after the initial shooting had ended. What was the scene?

MR. AND MRS. SMITH (1941)

Hitchcock purportedly was great friends with Carole Lombard, and all concerned had tons of fun making this film. The movie itself, some amusing lines notwithstanding, looks like warmed-over *The Awful Truth*, or *His Girl Friday*, complete with Ralph Bellamy role, in which sophisticated rich folk twist themselves into the most elaborate positions in order to avoid the simultaneous presence of two unmarried, unchaperoned people in the same city block. (All questions worth 10 points.)

For Questions 1–8, identify the following.

1. Krausheimer.

2. Harry Deaver.

3. Beefeater's Club.

4. Florida Club.

5. Mamma Lucy's.

6. Smith & Custer.

7. Lake Placid.

8. Beauchamp.

9. What is the question that starts all the trouble?

10. What was the technicality that un-married the Smiths?

Extra Credit

11. What famous practical joke did Carole Lombard pull on the director the first day of shooting?

SUSPICION (1941)

Hitchcock returned again to the quaint English life he knew so well for his fourth American film. *Suspicion*, shot completely in Hollywood, inhabits that oxygen-poor world of fox hunts on country estates and opulent balls in which folks (with names like McLaidlaw and Aysgarth) pick out appropriately pedigreed spouses with which to propagate the race. Poor Lina is her father's girl, worried that she'll give the old man a heart attack if she fixes herself up. A serious, horsey type, she's a latent swooner—witness the Academy Award–winning transmogrification at the delivery of Johnny's first telegram. Notice also her propensity for putting on and taking off her glasses at strategic moments, the latter mainly when she doesn't want to see something about Johnny. Cary Grant's first Hitchcock movie, *Suspicion* is pretty silly but a great deal of fun. (Each question worth 10 points or as indicated.)

For Questions 1–3, identify the following.

1. *Child Psychology.*

2. Beauchamp Hunt Ball.

3. Tangmore-by-the-Sea.

4. What is General McLaidlaw's wedding gift to the happy couple?

5. What does the General will to Lina?

6. How does Johnny lose his job with Captain Mahlbeck?

7. How does Beaky die? Why does Lina believe Johnny is possibly guilty? (Five points each.)

8. Where is Johnny during this incident?

9. What book does Johnny borrow from Isabel, the mystery writer? And why does Lina think this loan significant? (Five points each.)

10. What is the little trade secret Johnny wrangled from Isabel that throws poor Lina into an apoplectic fit? And where did Isabel find this secret out? (Five points each.)

Extra Credit

11. What are the reasons given (in the last two seconds of the movie) for Johnny's pursuit of Lina's insurance money and of Isabel's secret? (Five points each.)

12. What is the ending Hitchcock claimed he always wanted to give the film?

SABOTEUR (1942)

Another in a series of Hitchcock anti-Nazi films. Dressed up as *Son of the 39 Steps, Saboteur* is a rather perfunctory effort on Hitchcock's part, since, as nearly every source reports, the director was mightily resentful of Selznick, who had sold the film to Universal at a substantial fee. This meant a large profit for Selznick (none of which Hitchcock saw) and a tiny production budget at Universal for Hitchcock to work with. Pretty stodgy, but not without its moments. (All questions worth ten points or as indicated.)

1. Barry Kane is accused of setting one fire, pretends to set another and prevents a third conflagration. How so?

2. Why is Kane suspected of murder? What's the name of the victim? (Five points each.)

3. Pat Martin, Barry's love interest and Hitchcock's Madeleine Carroll figure: What is her profession? Where do we see her first? (Five points each.)

4. Points of departure: What clue leads Barry to Spring Valley?

5. What leads Barry to Soda City?

6. Fry, the saboteur, provides the impetus for Barry's flight across the country. Yet Barry does not see him between the coasts; what is Fry doing when Barry finally catches up to him?

7. How does Barry break his handcuffs?

8. Which circus freak wants to turn the fugitives over to the police?

9. What are the names of our two well-respected paragons of society who serve as Nazi spies? (Five points each.)

10. How does Barry play for time when he and Pat are surrounded at the ball?

Extra Credit

11. Who are the two participants in the film who later proved invaluable in the production of the *Alfred Hitchcock Presents* TV series? (Five points each.)

12. At which scene did the US Navy take umbrage?

13. What famous New York writer was conscripted to add dialogue to the picture?

SHADOW OF A DOUBT (1943)

We brook no hyperbole in our role as quiz-makers, but will let stand any assumption that this film is one of Hitchcock's three or four richest. It contains the inexplicable presence of evil in a place of inert and complacent wholesomeness, and the combined beauty and suffocation of small-town America—the word "ordinary" is used repeatedly, with many connotations. And there is the theme of the double (or the *Doppelgänger,* if you prefer), the intricate structure and visual pairings—there are two of everything—that Hitchcock really turns with virtuosity in *Strangers on a Train.* Modern audiences tend to titter at Uncle Charlie's somewhat verbose monologues, but we will submit that they are not at all unrealistic for a person whose view of humanity is so cynical it admits only the grotesqueness of human beings. We may all be that person in bits and pieces, carefully controlled and closely watched, as Jack Graham says, and brought to light in the smallest increments in moments of despair or in those flirtations with evil we think we are strong enough or sophisticated enough to survive. Not that that's what this quiz is about, exactly. (All questions worth 10 points or as indicated.)

1. What are the two moments of telepathy between Uncle Charlie and his niece that are pointed out near the beginning of the film? (Five points each.)

2. What town did Charles and Emma grow up in? (Two extra points for the address.)

3. What superstition of Joe's does Uncle Charlie immediately violate?

4. What gifts does Uncle Charlie bring to Ann, Roger, Joe and Emma? There are two gifts for Emma. (Two points for each gift.)

5. What is Emma's conception of Charles's profession?

6. What is the inscription on the ring that Uncle Charlie gives his niece?

7. Who was the ring's original owner, and where do we find out?

8. What two other scenes deal significantly with the ring? (Five points each.)

9. How many people has Uncle Charlie killed?

10. What was the childhood accident that almost killed Charles?

Extra Credit

11. Here in Small Town, America, you have your Wholesome Romance and your more sinful type, and their respective places of recreation. Where do Jack Graham and Uncle Charlie each take young Charlie on subsequent nights on the town? (Five points each.)

12. Who was Hitchcock's main collaborator on the film?

13. What significant personal tragedy did the Hitchcock family suffer during the filming?

LIFEBOAT (1944)

A lifeboat with nine people, flotsam from the sinking of a British passenger liner and a German U-boat, makes for the most restricted setting in a long line of restricted-setting experiments. Hitchcock meant it as a sort of war-effort allegory in which the majority of the passengers (their stations in life writ large with significance like characters in a wet *Pilgrim's Progress*) represent the Allies, divided and bickering and stifled by a lack of will, ineffectively set against the one iron-willed, unwavering Superman of a German, who rows the boat with the brute strength and stamina of a Clydesdale while the others bemoan their lack of same. It seems somehow, also, to stand up to a more subtle psychological explanation, especially given the ugliness and lack of triumph of the scene in which the Allies viciously beat the German and throw his body overboard. This ambiguity garnered the film a stormy reception in some quarters that were peeved at the suggestion that Germans had any admirable qualities or that the Allies had any unadmirable ones. (All questions worth 10 points or as indicated.)

1. Which lifeboat passengers fill these roles in their pre-lifeboat lives? (Two points each.)
   a. Steward.
   b. Engineer.
   c. Reporter.
   d. Radio operator.
   e. Captain.

2. After the German sailor climbs on board, a little straw poll is taken to determine whether or not to toss him back. Given that there are eight non-Teutonic passengers and (arguably) two abstentions, how does the vote go? Who are the two that don't vote? (Five points each.)

3. Where is Kovac's family from? What is Gus's real last name? (Five points each.)

4. Why is Alice MacKenzie not terribly heartbroken that she won't make it to England?

5. Connie Porter, cynical and worldly-wise, has her defenses stripped away along with the possessions she has managed to get into the lifeboat. Not counting her stockings, there are five of these precious items, all eventually winding up in the sea. Name them. (Two points each.)

6. Willy the German, conversely, seems to end up with more stuff as the story progresses: a compass, an understanding of English, a flask of water. . . . What incident gives away the fact that he speaks English?

7. What, other than the hoarded water, gives Willy the strength to keep rowing?

8. What incident finally makes the passengers turn on Willy? What gives him away? (Five points each.)

9. Kovac the communist (after a fashion) and C. J. Rittenhouse, the millionaire, play poker with a set of impromptu cards. What does Kovac plan to do with the money he has won?

10. The technical challenge for Hitchcock, as discussed earlier, was that the story would be shot in a single, incredibly small setting. So the camera never leaves the boat or the surface of the immediately surrounding ocean, except for once. What is this shot of?

Extra Credit

11. Identify: Reduco.

12. Who is Al Magarulian?

13. What small scandal did Tallulah Bankhead perpetrate on the set?

14. Whom did Hitchcock originally ask to write the script for *Lifeboat?*

15. What famous novelist contributed to an early version of the screenplay?

SPELLBOUND (1945)

A highly amusing film, often intentionally. In this Freudian melodrama the doors of perception open at the lovers' first kiss ("Unfortunately, the violins begin to play just then," Hitchcock said to Truffaut. "That was terrible.") and deep psychic prescriptions are filled with admonitions to call the shrink in the morning. This psychoanalytic patness (rather like a lot of New York dinner conversation, come to think of it) contains some interesting (and vital) questions about guilt in the human mind, etc., but this film will never be easily confused with, say, *Cries and Whispers*. As a matter of fact, it might be fun to combine *Spellbound* with *A Day at the Races*—Chico Marx hustling a confused Gregory Peck into his bus to become the new director of the sanitorium, Leo G. Carroll doing a slow burn while Peck repeatedly washes his hands during the surgery scene, Harpo drawing parallel lines on all the walls. . . . The Salvador Dali sequence, it is reported, was originally meant to be twenty minutes long, and involved turning Ingrid Bergman into a statue and then covering her with ants. (Each question worth 10 points or as indicated.)

1. Why is Dr. Murchison being relieved of his command?

2. Who are the two patients of Constance Petersen's that appear in the story, and what are their problems? (Five points each.)

3. The very well-regarded new head of the hospital, Dr. Edwardes, has written a fascinating new book. What is its title?

4. Name five objects or places that trigger our false Dr. Edwardes's fits. (Two points each.)

5. What is Constance's first clue—besides the constant swooning—that this Edwardes is an imposter?

6. What is Constance's clue as to Dr. Murchison's villainy? That is, what slip does Murchison make that enables Constance to connect him with the murder?

7. What is the childhood memory that John Ballantine has blocked, and what finally triggers this memory? (Five points each.)

8. The dream: What images in the dream are interpreted by Dr. Brulov as standing for (a) a revolver, and (b) the mountain Dr. Edwardes fell from? (Five points each.)

9. Also from the dream: Where did Ballantine witness a heated quarrel between Murchison and Edwardes? What was the name of the resort where Edwardes died? (Five points each.)

10. Identify the speaker: "In my business you have to be a bit of a psychologist."

Extra Credit

11. What was the name of the doctor who had the hots for an unresponsive Constance?

12. According to Rohmer and Chabrol in their book about Hitchcock, what original scheme about color film did Hitchcock and adaptationist Angus MacPhail harbor?

13. What Academy Award did the film end up with?

NOTORIOUS (1946)

At the climax of the war, Hitchcock divined not only the entrepreneurial uses of uranium but the immense recreational potential of South America for vacationing Germans after the war. One of the most emotional films Hitchcock ever made, *Notorious* is fated forever after to play on double bills with *Casablanca*—a feast of Ingrid Bergman's mouth and cheekbones. The story of a woman forced into a kind of prostitution for her country will emerge again with *North by Northwest*—also featuring Cary Grant, of course, with a shoe on another foot. Raymond Durgnat, in his book *The Strange Case of Alfred Hitchcock*, suggests it might be instructive to combine the two movies, making Cary Grant the seduction victim of his own evil twin. Or, better yet, these two could be combined with *Spellbound*, making Cary Grant a schizophrenic who occasionally assumes the identity of his once-murdered father figure, playing both sides of the fence until he tries to kill her and is forced to confront himself, wrestle himself to the floor and allow the personalities to fight for possession of his body. (All questions worth 10 points or as indicated.)

1. In what city does the film open, and in what year? (Five points each.)

2. What is Devlin's first name?

3. How does Alicia's father die?

4. Where did Alex Sebastian previously know Alicia?

5. What is Mrs. Sebastian's first bone of contention with Alicia, other than the fact that her son is attracted to her?

6. What first draws Alicia's attention to the bottles of wine?

7. How is Hupka killed? Why is he missed? (Five points each.)

8. What is inscribed on the key to the wine cellar?

9. What vintage is the bottled uranium?

10. When does Alicia know she is being poisoned?

Extra Credit

11. Kindly Dr. Anderson is working under an alias. What do the Americans know him as?

12. What is the American superior's name in Rio?

13. Who does Devlin purport to work for, as part of his cover?

THE PARADINE CASE (1947)

Hitchcock's last picture for Selznick, strictly a lame-duck affair, in which Gregory Peck, distinguished London barrister, accounts himself a fool for love, developing an obsessive fascination with the mysterious Mrs. Paradine and making everyone most uncomfortable in the process. Eventually he makes a great spectacle of himself in court and withdraws in disgrace—and none too soon, either. Selznick and Hitchcock's relationship was at its worst. When the producer felt that his director was dragging his heels on this important international picture of his, he took on the scripting job himself, compulsively rewriting scenes just as they were about to be shot. (All questions worth 10 points or as indicated.)

For Questions 1–4, identify the following:

1. The victim and the murderer. (Five points each.)

2. The family solicitor and the defense attorney. (Five points each.)

3. The motive for murder.

4. The means of murder.

5. What is most striking about Mrs. Paradine's bed?

6. What becomes the main defense tactic?

7. What incident does Keane come up with in an effort to prove Latour's proficiency with the means of murder?

8. What finally triggers the murderer's confession?

9. Judge Horfield turns out to be quite an unpleasant fellow. In addition to humiliating his poor wife at every opportunity, what does he do at his own dinner party that makes for a much uncomfortable ambience? To what does Horfield compare the human brain? (Five points each.)

10. What do Sir Simon and his daughter Judy argue about?

Extra Credit

11. What did Major Paradine have for his last meal?

12. What bad habit does beleaguered Gay Keane pick up as a result of her husband's obsession?

13. Why did Hitchcock bemoan the casting of Louis Jourdan as Latour?

14. How was Gregory Peck made to look at least somewhat more like an English barrister?

Photo Quiz II:
Precious Family Ties and Intimate Discussions

(All questions worth 10 points.)

1. What are these people looking at so ardently?
2. What is the significance of their observation?

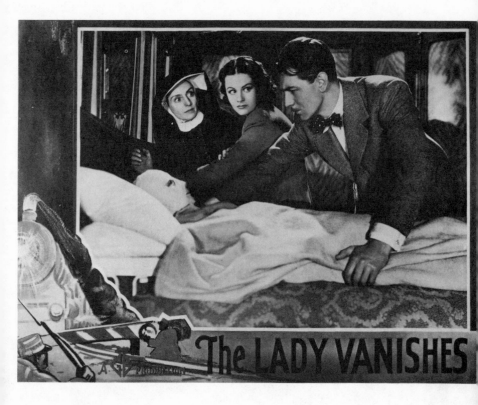

3. Who is the patient?

4. This gentleman is supplying a welcome second opinion. What had the patient's first doctor decided to do?

5. Visiting the relatives: What is the occasion?

6. How do the young couple manage to slip away from Erica's very inquisitive aunt?

7. What is not strictly kosher in this apparently comforting domestic scene?

8. Who is the kindly gentleman standing and what is his solution for Alicia's recent ill health? (Five points each.)

9. What is this woman suggesting to this child?

10. What song of questionable taste is being sung at this very moment?

The Fifties (1948–1959)

DEPENDING on whom you talk to, the 1950s were the years either of maturation or of cynical Hollywood-ization for Hitchcock. Obviously, we are going to take the former position. The fifties saw his greatest films and his happiest collaborations. Half of the Cary Grant and all of the James Stewart and Grace Kelly movies were made during these years, not to mention the inestimable *Strangers on a Train* (1951) and the amazing string of hits from *Rear Window* (1954) to *North by Northwest* (1959) that would make Hitchcock the most famous movie director in the world. We are starting this period, for the sake of convenience, with *Rope* (1948), as it makes a logical break in Hitchcock's career. *Rope* was his first independent production (free of the Selznick shackle) and represents a watershed of development and experimentation in his work. In addition to the success of his films, Hitchcock was also much celebrated and the recipient of not a few royalty checks as a result of his *Alfred Hitchcock Presents* TV shows and their very droll introductions by the director. The series started in 1955, and although just a handful of episodes were directed by Hitchcock himself in the ten years the show aired (in 1962 it became *The Alfred Hitchcock Hour*), the program helped make him not only the most well-known, but perhaps one of the world's richest filmmakers to boot. At this point we could insert the old title about riches and fame not being everything—probably the most casual viewing of *Vertigo* would make this obvious in Hitchcock's case—but just *how* it wasn't everything is a little beyond the ken of this

book. We refer the reader as always to Spoto's endlessly fascinating
The Dark Side of Genius, girding our loins meanwhile for the higher
type of scholarship to which we have been called.

ROPE (1948)

Warner Bros., screenplay by Arthur Laurents from the play by
Patrick Hamilton.

(All questions worth 10 points or as indicated.)
This is of course the famous exercise (a "stunt," Hitchcock called it)
in the theoretical single-shot movie, the presentation of a story in
real time apparently recorded by one camera in a continuous motion
without a single cut—an abrupt transfer from one object to another—although there are in fact *two cuts,* the first of which occurs
immediately after the credits and the second of which we will discuss presently. The story itself involves the murder of one David
Kentley by his school chums Philip and Brandon (whose sexuality,
addressed voluminously elsewhere, we will not discuss, except to
mention that the story is believed to be based on the Leopold and
Loeb case), and the subsequent party insisted on by Brandon (who
gives what *two reasons* during the course of the night for the gather-
ing?—*Question 1,* 5 points each reason). To this party are invited
David's parents, his fiancée Janet, his former best friend Kenneth
(who is invited for what perverse reason of Brandon's?—*Question
2*), and the party's *real* guest of honor—indeed, the man for whom
this whole show is being staged—Rupert Cadell, a former professor
of the boys' whose acerbic charm and intellect end up offending
David's father (how so?—*Question 3*). Strangely enough, Brandon,
although in awe of his (unintentional?) mentor, clearly feels superior
to him (why?—*Question 4*) and plays a game with him, dropping
hints all night that David might not show up, seeming to goad
Rupert into figuring out what they have done (and congratulating
them?), while poor Philip, gentler of constitution, gets more and
more manic with each passing moment, and each smirking hint from
Brandon. At one point Brandon begins to needle Philip about a
bizarre activity Philip engaged in during his youth (which Rupert

actually witnessed Philip executing, but which we've forgotten the nature of—*Question 5)*, a discussion which unsettles Philip enough; but then, after dinner (of what?—*Question 6)*, and after Mrs. Atwater (David's aunt, who came in lieu of his mother, and who is something of an amateur palm reader) tells a very curious fortune from his very tense palms (which we will ask as *Question 7)*, Brandon drives his friend near to apoplexy with his conceptual pièce de résistance—the production of the murder weapon for all to see (how does he do this?—*Question 8)*. Rupert of course cannot fail to notice all of this, and as the evening progresses he becomes increasingly afraid that something is terribly wrong (especially when he sees something in the closet that seems to indicate that David *was* there earlier—*Question 9)*, a fear that is so strong, he follows the other guests out but finds a pretext to return to the apartment *(Question 10a,* 5 points) and brings with him something that leads to all sorts of consternation *(10b,* 5 points). It is then that Rupert wrestles a gun away from the two men, figures out what has happened and summons the police by firing out the window, all the while pondering, as we are,

just where it was that that second cut, which we discussed earlier, came—that is, whom did the camera cut from and to (extra credit, *Question 11a,* 5 points) and what was being discussed *(Question 11b,* 5 points)? Also, just to tie up some loose ends, it occurs to us to ask what the piano piece Philip played during the evening was *(Question 12)*, what character we have heretofore forgotten to mention *(Question 13)* and just how long each individual take lasted during the filming of *Rope (Question 14)?*

UNDER CAPRICORN (1949)

Seldom seen and usually dismissed critically, *Under Capricorn* is actually pretty fascinating. There is a smoldering class resentment that Milly and Charles exacerbate from either end in their efforts to separate husband and wife. There is the typically Hitchcockian tyranny of the past (and the dead) over the present (and the living). And there is the understated theme of the way disappointment—

sadness—has a self-perpetuating inertia in an individual's life. The flight from England, the years Sam has spent in prison—and we have only a short, tantalizing account of how Henrietta spent those years—combined with rejection from a damnable proper Sydney society have poisoned things irrevocably for the lovers, introducing an element of the defeat that seems as if it can't be overcome. Interesting the way the word "gentleman" is used repeatedly: by turns glibly, ironically and bitterly. Also interesting is the way Charles becomes liberator, villain (the new Milly) and liberator again. (All questions worth 10 points or as indicated.)

1. What function did Sam Flusky perform with the Considine family?

2. What business deal does Sam strike up with Charles Adare at their first meeting?

3. How long had Flusky been in prison? Whose life had the murderous brother been threatening when Hattie killed him? (Five points each.)

4. Why does Sam ask Charles to dinner?

5. Charles had been Hattie's best friend's brother back in Ireland—little Charlie. What trait of his did Hattie remember, to the exclusion of just about everything else?

6. The perfidious Miss Milly "has a way" with her mistress, as Sam says. How does Milly keep Hattie at wit's end?

7. During Charles's renovation plan, how does Milly humiliate Hattie in front of the servants?

8. When Milly leaves, what "possession" of hers does Sam give to Hattie as a symbol of her new dominance over the household? What symbolic gesture does Hattie make in front of the servants to indicate the change of management? (Five points each.)

9. What incident triggers Hattie's confession to the governor?

10. What other character has had to pay in prison for loving unwisely?

Extra Credit

11. What year is the story set in?

12. What is the name of the Flusky estate—or the English translation, at least?

13. What small turmoil was commenced in Ingrid Bergman's life during the filming?

STAGE FRIGHT (1950)

At a crisis point in Hitchcock's career, after the technical experiments (and commercial failures) of *Rope* and *Under Capricorn*, one of the most conventional movies in the Hitchcock catalogue was quite lukewarmly received at the time. To be fair, whenever the suggestion "lukewarm" is thrummed against the side of the head, it is always Jane Wyman's face that appears in the mind's eye. Even when the point of the movie seems to be that Eve Gill becomes a better actress through the roles she is forced to play in a "real life" drama, we cannot help but think that she is just as bad at *that*. Still, there is no denying this film is exceedingly funny, and a great deal of fun. The movie is about "the folly of transmuting melodrama into real life," as the Commodore says, a symptom one is well aware of if one has ever become friendly with an actor. The supporting cast is extremely entertaining, especially when Marlene Dietrich lets go with one of her Elmer Fudd-isms. Also much discussed are the famous lying flashback and the film's clever theater imagery. (All questions worth 10 points or as indicated.)

1. What is the essence of Jonathan Cooper's lie?

2. Three of the most important confessional/expositional scenes take place in vehicles, among them Jonathan's flashback in Eve's car, and Eve's burgeoning romantic negotiations (and first kiss) with Smith in a taxi. Where, specifically, is the third such scene, when Jonathan tells Eve the truth about himself?

3. The Commodore, speaking to Eve of her "real life" melodrama, says, "You have a plot, an interesting cast—even a costume." What is the costume he refers to?

4. Who apparently is the current romantic interest in Charlotte Inwood's life?

5. What nickname does Smith prefer to his Christian name? And what *is* his Christian name, anyway? (Five points each.)

6. What is the name of the maid? What is the name of the pretend maid? (Five points each.)

7. How many performances does Charlotte miss in her role of grief-stricken widow?

8. The Commodore advances large doses of "the absence that makes the heart grow fonder" as the secret of success for what venerable institution?

9. It appears that young Jonathan is much more unstable than we originally presumed. This might qualify him to be a more successful actor, a success we would not begrudge him but for the fact that he has killed before. How did he beat the rap?

10. What is significant about the nature of the bloodstain on Charlotte Inwood's dress?

Extra Credit

11. What number is Charlotte singing when she is presented with the bloodstained doll? What is the other tune we hear all the way through?

12. What is significant about the character of Eve Gill, vis-à-vis the Hitchcock family in 1949?

STRANGERS ON A TRAIN (1951)

You will forgive your humble quizzer if at this point he is obliged to bite down on his tongue in order to quell his enthusiasm somewhat, for *Strangers on a Train* is a film that is so rich thematically and so . . . geometrical, that one who is not mathematically inclined may look on it with just a bit less awe than one would, say, a Bach fugue, or the concept of the space-time continuum. The film boasts not only a great performance by the doomed Robert Walker, some of the greatest dialogue to grace a motion picture (Man: "Smoochers won't go near the place since the murder." Bruno: "I'm afraid I don't know what a *smoocher* is." Man: "All right, so I ain't educated."), but also a marvelous structure. The theme of the double and the repetition of pairings are elements that have been admirably discussed in more informed quarters than these, and the reader who seeks out exegeses of this complex film will be well rewarded. It falls to us, however, to follow a more basic—even common—path to perfection. To wit: (All questions worth 5 points.)

1. The opening of the film introduces Guy Haines, the tennis star, and Bruno Anthony, who seems to know quite a bit about Guy. Does Bruno actually engineer the meeting?

2. The second line and the final line of the film are the same; what is said and by whom? (A big two extra points for the actual first line of the picture.)

3. What is the name of Guy's hometown?

4. Where does Miriam work?

5. What is inscribed on Guy's lighter?

6. Do Bruno and Guy speak between their encounter on the train and Miriam's murder?

7. What is the name of the island where Bruno kills Miriam?

8. What symbol of Guy's ambitions looms outside his apartment?

For Questions 9–13, identify the following.

9. "The Band Played On."

10. Delaware Tech.

11. Hennessey.

12. *Pluto*.

13. St. Francis.

14. As Bruno tries to convince Guy to carry out "his part" of their imagined bargain, he creeps further and further from the shadows into Guy's well-ordered life. List Bruno's attempts to nudge Guy in order:

   a. The phone call at the Mortons' house.

   b. The steps of the Jefferson Memorial.

   c. Across the street from Guy's apartment.

   d. A map and a key under Guy's door.

   e. Confrontation at the Capitol, with Ann.

   f. A Luger in the mail.

   g. Crashing the Mortons' party.

   h. Meeting Ann at the tennis club.

   i. A letter: "We must get together and make plans . . ."

15. How does Ann Morton, at the tennis club, recognize Bruno from a previous encounter?

16. The theme of the double and the playing around with visual pairs is often discussed, most obviously in the contrast of Guy and Bruno. To which other character is the murdered Miriam visually linked?

17. What proof does Bruno offer Guy of his successful murder?

18. Bruno confronts two little boys at the fairgrounds, one on each of his trips there. What happens in the first incident?

19. What happens in the second incident?

20. How many people die during the course of the film?

Extra Credit

21. What is Hitchcock carrying during his cameo appearance?

22. Hitchcock and Raymond Chandler, despite the many thematic similarities in their work, were uneasy collaborators, and the director claimed to have had much of Chandler's script redone. In Chandler's original version, what happens to the Bruno character?

23. What was the name of the night-duty cop?

I CONFESS (1953)

An overlooked little gem about guilt and faith and evil, in which Father Michael Logan is charged with a murder he did not commit, yet cannot defend himself against it because, as it happened, he had taken the killer's confession. A man to whom his parishioners look for guidance and strength, Father Logan is forever saying "I wish I could help you," and "I'm sorry, I'm just not able to help," mostly to lovesick women and zealous officers of the law. The film's lack of humor, its occasional ham-handed acting (which in Anne Baxter's case would seem to be the point; the melodrama of her misty, sentimental little face) and its stylization leave it open to scourging by callow youths in revival houses everywhere. But its themes and images give it a power that lingers and makes it richer through repeated viewings. Recommended reading is Rohmer and Chabrol's essay on *I Confess* and Donald Spoto's case in *The Dark Side of Genius* for Hitchcock's personal identification with both Logan and the killer, Otto Keller. (All questions worth 10 points or as indicated.)

1. What does Ruth Grandfort say to Logan on hearing of Villette's death?

2. How many blackmail payments had Ruth made to Villette?

3. What time does the coroner estimate as that of Villette's death? On what night of the week is he killed? (Five points each.)

4. How many people are killed or wounded in the film? Who are they?

5. Alma and Otto Keller both say the same thing as they are dying, which is:

6. What important logistical lie does Keller tell on the stand?

7. Willy Robertson, the Crown Prosecutor, is twice pointedly shown balancing objects. What is he balancing on these two occasions? (Five points each.)

8. Why does Ruth's confession to Larrue and Robertson fail to clear the air?

9. What is the name of Logan's parish? What city is the film set in? (Five points each.)

10. How long had it been since Ruth had seen Logan before the night of the murder? What was the last occasion? (Five points each.)

Extra Credit

11. Does the bloodstained cassock turn out to be a decisive element in the verdict?

12. Keller makes much of the fact that he is a stranger in the country, that he has no friends but his wife and Logan. After alienating Logan and killing Alma, obviously his circumstances have not improved drastically. But in their final confrontation Keller insists that Logan's situation is more pitiful than his own. Why?

13. According to all accounts, Hitchcock was most exasperated with Montgomery Clift during the shooting. One reason was Clift's out-of-control drinking. What was the other?

14. The original Ruth was to be Anita Björk, a Swedish actress much acclaimed at the time in her performance of *Miss Julie*. What happened to her?

DIAL M FOR MURDER (1954)

The Haineses of Metcalf are reprised (aged and gussied up some-what) as the Wendices of London—and the husband actively tries to kill his now inconvenient wife. This may be a slight little film, as is often said, but whose heart does not leap when the light from Margot's room floods the living room—or when Swan waits for her to lower the receiver away from her face so that he can slip the scarf around her neck? (All questions worth 10 points or as indicated.)

1. What is Tony Wendice's motive for having Margot murdered?

2. What time is the murder planned for?

3. Tony appears to be an astute judge of rotten character. What little scandal had Swan perpetrated when they were in school together at Cambridge?

4. How does Tony ultimately blackmail Swan, and what was the name of the party involved? (Five points each.)

5. What work has Tony been engaged in since his retirement from tennis? What does Mark Halliday do? (Five points each.)

6. Why were the scissors on the table?

7. The missing love letter from Mark to Margot is quite important to all concerned. Apparently it was the last of several. Why does Tony think the letters stopped?

8. The business of the latchkeys is ultimately the clue to providing the evidence for Margot's innocence. Where is Margot's latchkey during the investigation? Where is Swan's? (Five points each.)

9. What starts Inspector Hubbard snooping around again after Margot is convicted? Why does the confusion of latchkeys begin to take on significance for him? (Five points each.)

10. What has Margot decided to do at the beginning of the picture vis-à-vis her romantic situation?

Extra Credit

11. At the beginning of the story the lovers had not seen each other for a year. What did they have on their last meal a year before?

12. What gimmick did Warner Bros. foist upon Hitchcock as a marketing tool for the film?

13. What alias is Swan working under when we first meet him?

REAR WINDOW (1954)

To begin, we will examine the logistical factors of this inquiry (quite like memorizing a pre–Great War map of Europe the first week of a European Civ class). The scene is a Greenwich Village apartment in the 1950s on a sweltering, oppressive New York summer day. L. B. Jeffries looks across the courtyard from his rear window, spying on the routine goings-on of his neighbors, who are (1) a sculptress, (2) a childless couple with a small dog, (3) a musician, (4) a lonely woman, Miss Lonelyhearts, (5) Lars Thorwald, a traveling salesman, and bits of his missus, (6) two newlyweds and, (7) Miss Torso, a limber young thing. Questions 1–7 will require the participant to place each of these in their correct apartments as indicated by the letters on the photograph. (All questions worth 5 points or as indicated.)

8. What is written on Jeff's cast?

9. Excepting the epilogue, how many days does the story involve?

10. On what night does the murder take place?

11. What is Stella's occupation?

12. After Tom Doyle talks Jeff and Lisa out of their suspicions about Thorwald, what incident reawakens them?

13. What specific incriminating evidence does Lisa hope to find in Thorwald's apartment? Where does she hope to find it?

14. What is written on the note Lisa slips under Thorwald's door?

15. What significant development does Jeff miss by falling asleep?

16. What is in the trunk that Thorwald packed?

17. Where is Mrs. Thorwald supposed to have gone? What was written on the postcard Thorwald received?

18. How did Jeff break his leg?

19. What leads Jeff to suspect that there is something fishy about Thorwald's garden?

20. What does Thorwald assume is Jeff's motive for spying on him?

Extra Credit

21. Where is most of Mrs. Thorwald? Where is her head?

22. What street does Thorwald live on?

23. What was Mrs. Thorwald's first name?

TO CATCH A THIEF (1955)

If the reader is given to a lot of Hitchcock-related reading, which obviously we are (well, maybe not obviously, but we *are*), you will anticipate all the phrases we throw out in these introductions. "Sparkling entertainment" is one we may have picked out for *To Catch a Thief*, or Hitchcock's own "lightweight." "Not to be taken seriously" is the message usually implied. Okay, okay, but look, there is no denying this movie is *fun*—and it is moments like the catty confrontation between Brigitte Auber and Grace Kelly at the beach that make this film one of the most unself-conscious, un-forced—dare we say—articles of genius. It's Hitchcock's exercise in Zen flower arranging! For our taste, there is not a corny line present—and not a Gregory Peck or Jane Wyman to be seen. But plenty of Grace Kelly, luckily enough. (All questions worth 10 points or as indicated.)

1. What is John Robie's story? That is, (a) how did he become a thief, and (b) after he went to prison for it, what led to his release? (Five points each.)

2. Give two reasons why Robie's old Resistance pals (who all seem to work at Bertani's restaurant) might be resentful of our hero. (Five points each.)

3. Jessie and Frances Stevens, our American mother and daughter, "common folk with money" as Frances says, are vacationing in Monte Carlo. How did they come by their money?

4. Who arranges Robie's introduction to H. H. Hughson, the insurance agent? Who does Hughson work for? (Five points each.)

5. Who is responsible for the robberies Robie is being framed for? Who is the actual Robie imitator? (Five points each.)

6. Frances appears to know who Robie is from the beginning. Where did she first see him?

7. At some point it becomes clear that Robie's life is in danger. What note does he receive that points this out to him?

8. Why is it patently absurd that Foussard, the wine steward at Bertani's restaurant, should be accused of being the Cat?

9. Robie is aware of someone casing the Silvers villa, and is also aware that the Stevenses' jewels are being assessed for thievery. Someone has seen the list of their stones that Hughson gave him; how does he know?

10. What does Robie do, more or less, for an income?

Extra Credit

11. What name does Robie go by in his initial meetings with the Stevenses? What business is he allegedly in? (Five points each.)

12. There is an *International Herald Tribune* in Robie's home at

the beginning of the picture. Who wrote the story speculating about the return of the Cat?

THE TROUBLE WITH HARRY (1955)

We all know people like Harry Warp. "He was too good to live . . . horribly good," his sometime wife Jennifer says. But if it is true, as Bruno Anthony says, that some people are better off dead (and who can deny it?), some of those *same* people are just as much a pain in the ass dead as alive. Like Harry Warp. (All questions worth 10 points or as indicated.)

1. How many times is Harry buried and dug up in the course of the story?

2. How do Captain Wiles and Miss Gravely each believe they have killed him? (Five points each.)

3. What was Harry's itinerary during his last moments; that is, how did he receive two blows on the head and what was the explanation for his behavior toward Miss Gravely?

4. Why had Harry married Jennifer? Why did he prove so ineffectual on their wedding night? (Five points each.)

5. What do Jennifer, Arnie, Mrs. Wiggs, Captain Wiles and Miss Gravely each receive from the millionaire for Sam's paintings? (Two points each.)

6. What does Sam ask for?

7. What two pieces of evidence does Calvin Wiggs have to substantiate his suspicion of a dead man on the hill? (Five points each.)

8. What happens to the evidence?

9. How had Harry actually died?

10. Who has the first line of dialogue in the movie?

Extra Credit

11. What is the name of the town?

12. What does Arnie get for his dead rabbit?

13. What important collaborator of Hitchcock's started his longtime association with the director with *The Trouble With Harry?*

THE WRONG MAN (1956)

Christopher Emmanuel Balestreros' is one of the world's poor blessed meek, a pious taxpayer who does not drink or take any pleasures away from his family, for whom the most necessary medical bills are serious financial setbacks and whose wife cannot even afford to come see him play in his band. It is Hitchcock's most documentary film, in the sense of duplicating the principal identities and facts of the incident the film is based on—down to the Balestreros' street address. The movie elicits outrage on two levels—at the lazy kind of procedural police state (this happened thirteen years before the *Miranda* ruling) that takes advantage of Manny's naive belief in the rightness of the law, and at the hysteria (exhibited by the women in the insurance office) that unblocks a person's sense of fairness and endangers others' lives. Small recompense that the most infuriating of the office women gets slapped by Tippi Hedren in *The Birds*. (All questions worth 10 points or as indicated.)

1. Where does Manny earn his living? What instrument does he play? (Five points each.)

2. Why does Manny go to the insurance office?

3. Manny is accused of having robbed Associated Life on July 9 and December 18. Where was he on the first date? What do he and O'Connor come up with relating to the second date, that might prove he has been mistakenly identified? (Five points each.)

4. How many people can potentially give Manny an alibi for July 9? What has become of these people? (Five points each.)

5. Where do the cops drag Manny on the night of his arrest?

6. The police make Manny duplicate the holdup note that was given to the clerk at Associated Life. Besides the "rough similarity" in the block printing, what did the cops find incriminating about Manny's note?

7. The district attorney makes an unfounded accusation during the trial about why Manny needed money. What is it?

8. What causes the mistrial?

9. What does Manny hold during the trial? What is he doing when the real thief is apprehended? (Five points each.)

10. What does Manny say to the real thief when they meet in the police station?

Extra Credit

11. How many years was Rose in the asylum? Where did the family move after she got out? (Five points each.)

12. Where did the family live in New York?

13. On what date does the story begin?

VERTIGO (1958)

The mind reels at the task of playing Twenty Questions with a film as rich and troubling as Vertigo. One can read in many places how

autobiographical the movie probably was for Hitchcock, chock-full
as it is with such doomed romantic longing, guilt, obsession and
death. . . . It is nightmarish, unsettling work. Many are the film-
goers who writhe in a painful fascination while Jimmy Stewart re-
lentlessly transforms Kim Novak into the image of a dead woman
. . . and many are the live women, come to think of it, who shrink
from *this* film-goer's public company after being taken to see this
film. We could, if we were of half a mind (we are of slightly less than
that), discuss this movie half the night. Due to the recreational
nature of this enterprise, however, we shall quietly drop behind the
opinion leaders in the lead car (discussing exactly what Scottie's sin
was) and content ourselves with certain fun facts to know and tell.
(All questions worth 5 points or as indicated.)

1. Scottie and Midge were engaged for three weeks in school.
   Who broke it off?

2. How did Gavin Elster amass his fortune?

3. Carlotta Valdes: What relation does Elster claim Carlotta is to
   Madeleine? (Knowledge of the years of her birth and death
   dates certainly should be worth an extra 5 points.)

4. As Scottie follows Madeleine around on that first day, each stop
   she makes ends up having something to do with Carlotta. Explain the connection in each of these places: (a) the florist, (b)
   the cemetery, (c) the art gallery, (d) the hotel. (Two points
   each.)

5. Does Midge ever actually get a look at Madeleine/Judy Barton?

6. Scottie and Midge get a lot of the Carlotta story from Pop
   Liebel at the Argosy Book Shop. According to this story, what
   led to Carlotta's madness?

7. The fake Madeleine is so into her role that even as she is waking
   up (or, rather, pretending to wake up) after her jump in the
   Bay, in the first words we hear her speak, she is playing the mad
   Madeleine/dead Carlotta angle for all it's worth. What does she
   say aloud, apparently in her sleep, that Scottie hears from the
   living room?

8. What does Scottie explain to Madeleine is his profession?

9. What San Francisco landmark does Madeleine use to find Scottie's house?

10. Who insists on going to San Juan Batista, and why? And how does this fit into the Carlotta story? (Three points each.)

11. What does Scottie do immediately after Madeleine's death that reflects rather poorly on him during the inquest?

12. Whose grave does Scottie fall into during his dream?

13. Where is Scottie when he first sees Judy Barton?

14. What place is described by Judy as "our place"?

15. What finally triggers Scottie's recognition that "Madeleine" and Judy are actually the same woman?

16. What causes Judy's fall from the tower?

17. How many people fall to their deaths in this film?

18. How are the stories of Judy Barton and Carlotta Valdes similar?

19. How did Carlotta die? How old was she, according to Elster?

20. Where did Judy Barton grow up? (Ten extra points for the exact address.)

Extra Credit

21. Which major character did screenwriter Samuel Taylor add in adapting the film from the novel (*D'entre les morts*, by Boileau and Narcejac)?

22. How did Hitchcock get the trick shot that visualizes Scottie's vertigo on the mission steps?

23. Whom did Hitchcock originally plan to cast as Madeleine, and what happened to her?

NORTH BY NORTHWEST (1959)

One of the most oft-viewed Hitchcocks, this little film holds a dear place in the heart of yours truly, as it was pretty directly responsible for sparking an adolescent obsession with the director's work that has outlived even the writing of this book. The film is much discussed for its summation of many Hitchcock ideas—the wrong man, the disruption of complacency by chaos, the problem of identity, the chase across country (the "picaresque" element, for those of you with pipes), the introduction of danger into symbols of order (the United Nations, Mount Rushmore)—that sort of thing. Also much discussed is the famous Cary Grant versus crop duster sequence, which of course loses much of its suspense after repeated viewings but none of its beauty. The popularity of $N \times NW$ leaves it open for a more-detailed-than-usual questioning, and, accordingly, this will be one of our more picky chapters. So saying (all questions worth 5 points or as indicated):

1. What is Roger Thornhill's profession?

2. What is Thornhill attempting to do when he is mistaken for George Kaplan?

3. Where is the Townsend mansion that Roger is taken to?

4. As the story progresses, Thornhill is forced to allow himself to assume the nonexistent Kaplan's identity—but when does he first *identify* himself as Kaplan?

5. There is much drinking done by Thornhill in the movie—in fact it is rather appropriate that he got drunk that evening at Townsend's place, as it is likely what he would have done anyway. In any case, match up the beverage Roger drinks with the location of said drinking below (1 point per correct answer):

   a. Gibson   1. The Oak Bar, Plaza Hotel.

   b. Bourbon.   2. The cafeteria at Mount Rushmore.

   c. Martini.   3. On the train.

d. Coffee.   4. Eve's hotel room.

e. Scotch.   5. Townsend's library.

6. Thanks to Leonard, who makes the selection, bourbon sort of becomes George Kaplan's drink. When, after he has finally adopted the identity of Kaplan, does Roger order bourbon?

7. Even after the expedient use of Kaplan's name throughout the story, Roger insists on his real identity in Vandamm's presence—until which scene?

8. What is the Professor's explanation of Vandamm's profession?

9. Where does Roger pick up that photograph of Vandamm—whom he still thinks is Townsend?

First impressions (Questions 10–12):

10. What is Leonard doing when we first see him?

11. What is Roger's first clue that all is not kosher with Eve?

12. Where does Roger first see Eve and Vandamm together?

13. The scene in Eve's compartment on the train contains a rather mincing dialogue, truth be told, until the revelation of Eve's involvement with Vandamm. What does her note to him say?

For Questions 14–15, identify the following:

14. Hwy. 41.

15. ROT.

16. What does the "O" stand for in the above?

17. In what state does the crop duster scene take place?

18. What proof does Leonard, who learns the truth about Eve, offer Vandamm of her treachery?

19. Why does Eve agree to go on the plane with Vandamm, even after she knows she has been exposed?

20. How many days does the basic story (excepting the epilogue) cover?

Extra Credit

21. What is George Kaplan's itinerary of hotels and cities during the course of the film? (Rememberers of a room number may feel especially smug and award themselves, say, 2 points.)

22. How many people die in the film?

23. What relation is Vandamm to "Mrs. Townsend"?

24. Interesting that the *real* antagonists of this story, the Professor and Vandamm, don't meet until the end. What is the only line of dialogue spoken between them?

25. Complete the following appropriately: "In advertising there is no such thing as a lie, there is only _____."

26. What is the probable classical reference in the film's title?

Photo Quiz III:
Drawing Blood on the Right Side of the Brain

(All questions worth 10 points or as indicated.)

1. Who is *not* being assassinated, all evidence to the contrary notwithstanding? And in what city? (Five points each.)

2. What does Johnny Jones find out is the reason for this little exhibition?

3. Alice White and the creative impulse: What sign of her presence does Alice erase before her departure for the evening? What sign of her presence does she leave behind? (Five points each.)

4. What is the significance of the dress on the left? How do Alice and the artist end their evening together? (Five points each.)

5. In whose house are the young couple honeymooning?

6. What has John seen that has upset him? What objection does he
   have to Constance's bedspread? (Five points each.)

7. Why does Philip here look so distraught at Rupert's reappearance?

8. What two uses has this piece of rope been put to during the evening?

9. Where is this woman?

10. Why is she standing before the end of the movement?

Murder Theme Quiz

A short investigation as to means of murder, victims and perpetrators. (All questions worth 5 points.)

Part I

Match up the victims with their appropriate mates.

1. Arbogast
2. Emile Hupka
3. Gus
4. Juanita de Cordoba
5. Annabella Smith
6. a lecherous artist
7. Patience Merlyn
8. Mr. Memory
9. Alma Keller
10. a friendly sailor

a. Rico Parra
b. Alice White
c. Norman Bates
d. Otto Keller
e. Marnie Edgar
f. Eric Mathis
g. agents of the 39 Steps
h. Willy
i. Professor Jordan
j. Squire Pengallan

Part II

Hitchcock's apparent favorite method, asphyxiation. Supply a victim for each convenient agent of strangulation or suffocation.

11. Necktie.

12. Oven.

13. Hands.

14. Rope.

15. Belt.

Part III

People to whom we have not been properly introduced. How did the following people die?

16. The Shoebridges.

17. Dr. Edwardes.

18. Villette.

19. Charlotte Inwood's husband.

20. Edna Druce.

Extra Credit

21. Who is killed with a fire extinguisher?

22. At two points apiece, name any individual who has either been hit by a stray shot or killed incidentally to the plot.

23. What man was shot and then stabbed, and died both times?

Quotes Quiz II

Identify the film and speaker or actor for each of the following. (All questions worth 5 points.)

1. "Why, the man's a half-caste!"

2. "Here, hold them . . . they're the most beautiful thing in the whole world, and the one thing you can't resist."

3. "I have my good points. People like me. I like flowers, and . . . fruit."

4. "I'm keen on golden curls myself, just like the Avenger."

5. "Go away or I'll kill you. I'll kill you myself. See? That's the way I feel about you."

6. "Talk about dream worlds! You've got a pathological fix on a woman who's not only a criminal but who screams if you come near her."

7. "I'm married to an American agent."

8. "Let me go—I've got kids—I didn't hurt anybody."

9. "Most girls would give their eyes to see Monte." "Wouldn't that rather defeat the purpose?" (Two speakers, one film.)

10. "I still think it's wonderful to have a man love you so much he'd kill for you."

11. "I'll buy you a mirror—it'll be your conscience."

12. "I always think of my murderers as my heroes."

13. "You gentlemen aren't really trying to kill my son, are you?"

14. "It's murder and you call it fun."

15. "He was too good to live. Horribly good."

16. "Give me an expense account and I'll cover anything."

17. "Call it my woman's intuition if you will, but I've never trusted neatness. Neatness is always the result of deliberate planning."

18. "I assume the supply of linen at this institution is inexhaustible."

19. "Then his body went limp. I knew it was all over. I felt a tremendous sense of exhilaration."

20. "East Berlin—why, that's behind the Iron Curtain!"

The Final Years (1960–1976)

THE years from 1960 to 1976, culminating with the release of *Family Plot,* his last film, were ones of increasing insecurity and disappointment for Hitchcock. From the popular heights of *Psycho* to the critical nadir of *Topaz* (which, we will argue later, is still pretty entertaining), with some intense personal devils thrown in, the period was sometimes horribly painful for the director, his wife Alma and their colleagues. As has been often discussed, most of the last films displayed an unremitting chill, a bleakness like that of the abandoned stretch of highway the Bates Motel is set on, that was not offset, as it may have been in the past, by the Happy Ending or by Hitchcock's instinct for creating popular entertainment. The somberness that reigns from *The Birds* through *Topaz* is nearly unrelenting, and the humor that informs *Psycho* and *Frenzy* is not exactly of your life-affirming Frank Capra variety. Ironically, the deal with Universal that Hitchcock struck—the same deal that made him incredibly rich—may have been one of the elements that hurt him the most, bringing handcuffs of corporate control along with financial security. Still, whatever else is said, these years saw the brilliant *Psycho* and *The Birds*—touchstones for a generation, if we may be so bold. And, luckily, Hitchcock's career ended on an upswing, with *Frenzy* and the friendly *Family Plot.* Toward the end of his life, everyone seemed most relieved and happy to have him around to honor with life-achievement awards and chuck honorary degrees at. And as unhappy as he may have been, he left a lifetime of formidable movies for the world to debate, marvel over and write quiz books about.

PSYCHO (1960)

Mother . . . uh, what is the phrase? She isn't quite herself to-day.—Norman Bates

When I leave the bathroom, everything is so clean you'd never know anyone had been in there.—Alfred Hitchcock

(All questions worth 4 points or as indicated.)

1. In what city does the opening scene of *Psycho* take place? (Two extra points to the especially observant for date and time.)

2. How much money does Marion Crane steal, and how much of it does she spend? (Two points each.)

3. What becomes of the money?

4. Who stares at Marion from a picture on her mantel at home?

5. What two people make Sam Loomis sweat? (Two points each.)

6. How old was Norman when his father died?

7. What do Norman and Mother argue about within Marion's hearing?

8. According to town legend, how did Mrs. Bates die?

9. What is the only scene in which we see Norman and Mother together?

10. According to Norman, how did the motel come to be built?

11. Why does no one come to the motel?

12. What name and hometown does Marion sign in the motel registry? (Two points each.)

13. What cabin does Norman give Marion? How many cabins are there? (Two points each.)

14. What is Norman's hobby? How has Mother contributed to his proficiency? (Two points each.)

15. To what suggestion of Marion's does Norman react angrily?

16. What covers up the peephole in Norman's office?

17. What are the first words spoken after Marion's murder?

18. What is a customer trying to buy in Sam's store when the scene opens there?

19. Why does Norman banish Mother to the fruit cellar?

20. Identify: periwinkle blue.

Questions 21–23 are multiple choice.

21. During Lila's search of the house, what does she see on Mother's bed?
    a. A stuffed cat.
    b. The indentation of a human form.
    c. A knife.
    d. A half-eaten sandwich.
    e. A jewelry box adorned with a pair of crossed hands.

22. What record does Lila find on Norman's phonograph?
    a. "Come On-a My House."
    b. "When You Wish Upon a Star."
    c. "Mad About the Boy."
    d. Polovtsian Dance No. 3 by Borodin.
    e. "Eroica" Symphony, movements 1 and 2 by Beethoven.

23. What kind of establishment does Sam Loomis run?
    a. A sweatshop.
    b. A hardware store.
    c. A pet shop.
    d. A luncheonette.
    e. A taxidermist's.

24. Who utters the line, "I'll take it out of her fine, soft flesh?"

25. How many days elapse from the opening of the film to the climactic scene in the fruit cellar?

Extra Credit

26. In which scene is the up-and-walking "Mother" not played by Tony Perkins?

27. What did Hitchcock use for blood in the shower scene?

28. What was the name of the operator in Fairvale?

29. What does Marion flush down the toilet?

THE BIRDS (1963)

Melanie Daniels in her gilded cage; the interruption of complacency by chaos; the sudden and violent inversion of the natural order. . . . As is often pointed out, *The Birds* is merely the culmination of Hitchcock's use of birds to symbolize chaos and destruction throughout his work, most significantly in *Psycho*. Something has changed with *Psycho*, which was fun; this one is really chilly, almost nihilistic. The final attack scene, with Tippi Hedren in the attic, took a whole grueling week to film, begloved bird handlers hurtling the animals at her repeatedly. A day's shooting concentrated on the last few seconds, Hedren covered with birds, strings tied to their feet and fastened through her clothes so that they would not walk away. Hitchcock mapped out an intricate structure on huge brown sheets of paper on his office walls—the rising and falling of action, scenes of confession and vulnerability followed by renewed attacks. The movie is marred only by some hammy acting, the stereotypes in the café, and poor Veronica Cartwright, who has to spend half the movie looking as if she's crying by squinting her eyes and opening her mouth wide. Like *Psycho*, this film is a milestone with a whole generation of people, a terrifying, enthralling peek at a world outside family and school and immediately surrounding blocks of safe suburban houses. (All questions worth 5 points or as indicated.)

1. What have Mitch Brenner and Melanie Daniels each come to Davidson's Pet Shop to buy?

2. How did Mitch know Melanie?

3. How did Melanie subsequently find out Mitch's name?

4. How did Melanie find out *Cathy's* name?

5. With Melanie's arrival in Bodega Bay, the bird attacks begin, singly at first, but soon escalating. Place the scenes of the attacks listed below in order. (One point per right answer.)

    a. The schoolyard.

    b. The house, through the chimney.

    c. The attic.

    d. The powerboat.

    e. The boarded-up house.

    f. The town.

    g. Annie Hayworth's door.

    h. The birthday party.

6. For each of the above, what kind of bird is the primary attacker? A hint, to be fair: two of the incidents were cooperative ventures between two types of birds. (One point each.)

7. Lydia Brenner and Annie Hayworth both have the same reaction to the news that Melanie has brought lovebirds to Cathy. What do they say?

8. What does Melanie's father do? What's the story with her mother? (Two points each.)

9. How long has Frank Brenner been dead? What attribute of his, other than his lack of hysteria, does his widow regret not having herself? (Two points each.)

10. What little escapade of Melanie's is Lydia evidently familiar with from the newspapers? What is Melanie's explanation? (Two points each.)

11. How long has it been since Annie Hayworth started coming to Bodega Bay? Why did she move there from San Francisco? (Two points each.)

12. Melanie is contrasted pointedly with Annie, in form as well as personality: their hair, their clothing, the colors associated with each of them. What is Annie doing when Melanie first pulls up to her door?

13. What three things does Melanie do with her week? (One point each.)

14. Why does Lydia go to Dan Fawcett's farm?

15. What is the name of the café in Bodega Bay?

16. The scene in the café before and during the attack on the town presents us with a nice little interaction of stereotypes; the rational scientist, the Irish drunk, the hysterical mother. . . . What theory does our hysterical mother advance to explain the presence of the birds?

17. What is the drunk's explanation?

18. What solution does the bellicose businessman have for the problem? And what becomes of this fellow?

19. What days of the week does the story begin and end on?

20. Curiosity killed the cat, or so they say; how does it prove similarly fatal to Annie Hayworth?

Extra Credit

21. What was the name of the machine built to simulate the electronic bird sounds on the sound track?

22. How old is Cathy?

MARNIE (1964)

We're going to stick up for *Marnie* against its many detractors—to a certain point, that is (though somewhat short of asserting that back-projection shots of Marnie riding happily are depictions of the unreality of her sense of freedom, or whatever that argument is). The film remains endlessly fascinating, though sometimes only partly due to the story we're seeing. We will not relate the unfortunate circumstances attending the making of this film—detailed in Spoto's biography—except to note that *Marnie* was obviously an obsession with Hitchcock and that whatever scars led up to and resulted from the filming were very deep. Added to this sadness was that this picture marked the end of Hitchcock's association with his trusted cinematographer Robert Burks and his editor George Tomasini (who both died before *Torn Curtain* was made) and longtime Hitchcock composer Bernard Herrmann, with whom there was a very unfortunate rupture of communication. (All questions worth 10 points or as indicated.)

1. What business is Mark Rutland in? Who is Strutt? (Five points each.)

2. Who is Lil Mainwaring?

3. What is the first cause of Marnie's swooning?

4. Marnie apparently has quite a history of thefts. What chance encounter threatens her (relative) security with Mark?

5. Lil finds out what is going on. How does she attempt to bring things to a head?

6. What possession of Mark's first wife is broken during the course of the story, and what is Mark's reaction? (Five points each.)

7. What does Marnie say both after the killing of her horse and the memory of the killing of the sailor?

8. What mark does Mrs. Edgar still carry from that encounter with the sailor?

9. Who is Marnie's chief rival for the affection of her mother?

10. What is the name of Marnie's horse?

Extra Credit

11. Who was the original screenwriter for *Marnie*, and what precipitated his falling-out with Hitchcock?

12. Whom did Hitchcock originally intend for Tippi Hedren's role?

TORN CURTAIN (1966)

Hitchcock's fiftieth film is generally regarded as a non-milestone in his career, but to tell the truth, it doesn't look half bad now, some clumsy cold war-isms ("East Berlin—why, that's behind the Iron Curtain!") and its (slightly) inappropriate principal actors notwithstanding. It does have, after all, probably the most intriguing Mac-Guffin (all that fascinating scribbling on Lindt's chalkboard) and one of the greatest murder scenes in all of filmdom. And Julie Andrews doesn't sing, which is much more than we could say for Doris Day in a similar situation. (All questions worth 10 points or as indicated.)

1. What was Michael Armstrong attempting to develop in Washington? And what was the name of the project in Washington? (Five points each.)

2. What organization is headed toward what city for its convention? (Five points each.)

3. What does the telegram that reaches Michael on board ship say?

4. What is the name of the resistance group? Where do we see the first reference to the group's name? (Five points each.)

5. Where did Gromek pick up his supply of American phrases? What is the final impetus in the decision to kill the poor fellow? (Five points each.)

6. What is Michael's cover story to Sarah when he is preparing to fly to East Berlin?

7. The ballerina turns out to be quite a nuisance. Where do we first see her? How does she twice prove to be trouble? (Five points each.)

8. Where do we see each of the following friendly agents: Koska, Albert, Hugo and Jacobi? What point of contact with π in Berlin does not quite pan out as planned? (Two points each.)

9. The Leipzig–Berlin bus makes four unscheduled stops. What are they? What was the name of the hysterical woman who objected to Michael and Sarah's presence? (Two points each.)

10. What is the most notable difference between Michael's experiments and Professor Lindt's?

Extra Credit

11. Where is the ballet company from?

12. The introduction of fire, or its suggestion, saves Michael and Sarah's hide on two occasions. What happens in both situations? (Five points each.)

13. Whose completed score was not used with the film, and why? (Five points each.)

TOPAZ (1969)

The nadir of Hitchcock's critical reputation (at least since coming to America), *Topaz,* with its tailored forces of good fighting the loud and sloppy forces of evil, is even fuller of trite cold war-isms than *Torn Curtain*. Still, like the previous film, it looks much better now than it probably did then, and is quite entertaining, despite its TV miniseries pallor, its occasional crises of self-confidence (Samuel Taylor was writing the scenes only days before they were shot) and its confusing statement of purpose—does Hitchcock mean to say that the Americans know what's best for everybody? Or that even the noblest causes take terrible tolls in human life? Or doesn't it matter? Probably not. (All questions worth 10 points or as indicated.)

1. What is Topaz?

2. Name the five places the action is centered in. (Two points each.)

3. What is the historical event that serves as background for the story?

4. What does Michael Nordstrom ask of Dévereaux while André is on vacation?

5. What is Luis Uribe's position? Why does he hate Americans? (Five points each.)

6. What two factors keep Juanita de Cordoba relatively immune from government surveillance? (Five points each.)

7. How does Dévereaux sneak his film out of Cuba?

8. What was Kusenov's position in the USSR? What is Henri Jarré's in Paris? (Five points each.)

9. Identify: a. Columbine; b. Den Permanente. (Five points each.)

10. Of what significance is the phone number BABYLON–8583?

Extra Credit

11. One of the things that made this film so traumatic for Hitchcock was the absence of an ending, up until (and beyond, as it happened) the end of shooting. What were the two previous endings filmed? (Five points each.)

12. What makes the final ending, Granville's suicide, particularly awkward from the standpoint of the film's production?

FRENZY (1972)

A disturbing, chilly, *mean* movie, this *Frenzy*. Also incredibly funny. It's the kind of picture you recommend to friends, who come out horrified and refuse to have any further dealings with you. After a long dry spell, *Frenzy* was Hitchcock unblocked, the intense gush of a truly misanthropic vision—a kind of testament to the sourness of mankind. Also, a tone poem of sorts about one of the director's greatest loves: food. Food jokes abound—"Don't squeeze the goods till they're yours," advises Bob Rusk, who proceeds to do just that. This film features a transference of guilt that doesn't ring true, a Wrong Man who is not strictly likeable, and probably one of the most gruesome murder scenes ever filmed (occasioning more squirming in the seat than a Rodgers and Hammerstein musical). Patricia Hitchcock reportedly would not let her family see it. A sick film, truly fascinating. (All questions worth 10 points or as indicated.)

1. Which section of London is the film centered in?

2. What two men—besides Bob Rusk and Richard Blaney, obviously—own a tie identical to the one the first murdered woman wears? (Five points each.)

3. Where does Blaney spend the first four nights of this story? What was the name of the specialty room at the hotel? (Two points each.)

4. Both Blaney and Rusk are tied, rightly or wrongly, to a murder by a powder or dust. What was this powder in each case, and how did it indicate (to the police at least) that the killer had had contact with his victim? (Five points per powder.)

5. What endearing comment does Rusk make to his victims?

6. On what grounds did Brenda Blaney obtain her divorce?

7. What does Bob Rusk (who does, as he says, have his "admirable qualities") describe as "frugal and mean"?

8. Where is Inspector Oxford's wife taking classes?

9. At one point Blaney and Babs have a plan of escape from London. What is it?

10. Where did Blaney and Johnny Porter (and probably Bob Rusk) know each other?

Extra Credit

11. What do the Jack Sprat-ish couple that we see at the Blaney Bureau ("Friendship and Marriage") have in common?

12. What is the name of the horse "Uncle Bob" gives Blaney a tip on?

13. What does Mrs. Oxford fix for Sergeant Spearman?

14. Who wrote a musical score for *Frenzy* that was never used?

FAMILY PLOT (1976)

Hitchcock's very last film, not with a bang but with a wink. A lightweight film, entertaining but a bit overplayed comically; by all accounts, the director at the end of his life was a very tired man. Still, there are touches of the old flash, and the slightly submerged theme of the pressure of the dead upon the living forms a link with Hitchcock's entire body of work. Unfortunately, there is a potentially great theme cursorily treated—the spawning of a monster child. Eddie Shoebridge/Arthur Adamson, a male Lizzie Borden with a psychopathic hatred of his past, takes a fiendish glee in kidnapping his onetime spiritual taskmaster, murdering his adoptive parents ("the happiest day of my life") and reading of old pal Maloney's death. Yet not one word in this film about the emotional problems of foster children. (All questions worth 10 points or as indicated.)

1. What is the problem with Eddie Shoebridge's grave? What is queer about its headstone? (Five points each.)

2. Who is disturbing Julia Rainbird's sleep, and what is her problem? (Five points each.)

3. What is Arthur Adamson convinced is Blanche and George's reason for pursuing him? And why is he so uneager to have his former identity exposed? (Five points each.)

George's progress in the investigation is measured by the acquiring of names. In Questions 4–6, where does he hear the following names for the first time?

4. Shoebridge.

5. Joe Maloney.

6. Arthur Adamson.

7. How many years after Eddie's "death" did he attempt, through Maloney, to have himself pronounced dead?

8. Maloney is keen on eliminating George as soon as he meets him, but Adamson decides to wait and investigate. What changes Adamson's mind fairly soon afterward?

9. What is the potential clue to her nephew's whereabouts that Julia Rainbird does not remember until after George's initial detective work?

10. What is the name of Blanche's spirit-world contact?

Extra Credit

11. What was the name of the Rainbird chauffeur?

12. What's the name of the café where Blanche and George are supposed to meet Maloney?

13. Who was originally cast in the William Devane role?

14. What was the title of the film up until its last stages of production?

Photo Quiz IV:
The Bosom of Justice and Other Interesting Places

(All questions worth 10 points.)

1. Where are all of these people?

2. What will shortly happen to Mr. Fry, at bottom right?

3. Who is visiting this office?

4. What very odd thing does he find out?

5. What has this man dropped?

6. Why can't he do without it?

7. Whose clothes are these?

8. Why does this man have them?

9. Who is this man, and why is he lying down?

10. What three people end up with this man's shoes?

The Wrong Man Theme Quiz

SUBMITTED for your approval: one of the major Hitch-cockian themes, involving an innocent man wrongly accused of a crime—a murder, say, or some other social gaffe. Suddenly these Wrong Men are thrown into a chaotic world that shatters their own secure one and are compelled to search for the guilty party at their own time and expense, and often at considerable personal risk. (All questions worth 4 points.)

For Questions 1–5, match up the appropriate Wrong Man with the real perpetrator of the crime he is accused of and the movie they both inhabit.

1. Michael Logan	Professor Jordan	*To Catch a Thief*
2. Barry Kane	Bob Rusk	*I Confess*
3. Richard Hannay	Otto Keller	*Frenzy*
4. John Robie	Fry	*Saboteur*
5. Richard Blaney	Danielle Foussard	*The 39 Steps*

Questions 6–7 deal with *North by Northwest*.

6. What is the Wrong Man's wrong name?

7. What *two* things is our Wrong Man accused of? (Two points each.)

Questions 8–9 deal with *The Wrong Man*.

8. What is Manny Balestrero, a mild-mannered musician by evening, accused of?

9. How is the real villain caught?

Questions 10–11 deal with *To Catch a Thief*.

10. How is Robie being framed for the series of jewel heists that the police have him pegged for?

11. What connection does the real thief have with Robie's former life of crime?

Questions 12–13 deal with *I Confess*.

12. What keeps Michael Logan from revealing the identity of the murderer?

13. What motive have the police assigned to Logan for his alleged murder?

Questions 14–15 deal with *Saboteur*.

14. What is Barry Kane accused of sabotaging?

15. How does Kane know the name of the real saboteur?

Questions 16–17 deal with *The Lodger*.

16. What possession does the Lodger have in common with the murderer, and how does an examination of this possession look very incriminating for him? (Two points each.)

17. What does the cop Joe Betts have to gain (besides a promotion, of course) by exposing the Lodger as the Avenger?

Question 18 deals with *The 39 Steps*.

18. What exactly *is* it that Richard Hannay is accused of, anyway?

Questions 19–20 deal with *Young and Innocent*.

19. What distinguishing physical characteristic does the murderer have?

20. What is Scotland Yard's sole piece of physical evidence against Robert?

Questions 21–22 deal with *Frenzy*.

21. Who are the two victims and what are their relationships to Richard Blaney? (One point each.)

22. Who finally betrays Blaney into the hands of the police?

23. What item of apparel do the Wrong Man and the villain share in both *The Lodger* and *The Wrong Man*, much to the confusion of local authorities?

24. What Wrong Men, in the films discussed above, do not wear handcuffs?

25. What Wrong Man, in a film *not* discussed above, imagines his own guilt for a murder he did not commit?

Extra Credit

26. In *North by Northwest*, how is the Right Man's namesake a victim of the Right Man?

27. In both *The Lodger* and *Frenzy* the Wrong Men are innocent of the crimes attributed to them, but what crimes of their own are they planning?

28. What wrong man is murdered by the heroes in a non–Wrong Man picture?

29. In which film, not mentioned above, does an apparent Wrong Man turn out to be the Right Man?

The MacGuffin Theme Quiz

FOR the majority of overeducated Hitchcock watchers, the term MacGuffin will come as no surprise. There is of course that humorous story about hunting lions in the Scottish highlands with a MacGuffin ("But there are no lions in the Scottish highlands." "Then that's no MacGuffin.")—you remember that one. But for the purpose of proper cataloguing in the Library of Congress, a MacGuffin is a Hitchcockian device used to initiate the plot that quickly becomes secondary (or even tertiary) to the thing that we really care about, the fate(s) of our hero(es). Mix and match, at your leisure, the underlying films and their corresponding MacGuffins. (All questions worth 10 points.)

1. *North by Northwest*

2. *The 39 Steps*

3. *Psycho*

4. *Notorious*

5. *The Lady Vanishes*

a. Exposure for a series of thefts

b. Wine bottles filled with uranium

c. A little old lady and a little old tune

d. Assassination of a public figure

e. A Tarrascan Warrior filled with microfilm

6. *Marnie*   f. Formula for an
                                                  antimissile missile

7. *Foreign Correspondent*   g. Specifications for British
                                                  fighter planes

8. *To Catch a Thief*   h. A little old man and
                                                  his secret

9. *The Man Who Knew Too Much*   i. A sum of unbanked
                                                  stolen money

10. *Torn Curtain*   j. A series of jewel heists

Extra Credit

11. How are the MacGuffin-ish services of our little old man and little old lady, mentioned above, similar?

12. According to Hitchcock legend, who came up with the term MacGuffin?

The End-of-the-Book Quiz

A more or less stream of consciousness exercise for the slightly advanced, in which lots of themes are touched on briefly. (Point values assigned accordingly.)

1. Name at least five films that end with one or multiple falls. (Two points each.)

2. Two films in which a villain looks as if he is about to read a note from the hero to the heroine, but doesn't, luckily. (Two points each.)

3. At least four portraits of dead people. (Two points each.)

4. Two men, dastardly ones, who fake limps. (Two points each.)

5. Special props: a big wooden finger, a big mechanical hand, and two huge glasses of brandy. Name the film that goes with the prop. (Two points each.)

6. At least three people who die on stages or in theaters. (Two points each.)

7. Two who die in a carnival or circus. (Two points each.)

8. Two villains who fix drinks after the jig is up. (Two points each.)

9. Two matrons in Monte: a cigarette in the cold cream, and a cigarette in the eggs. (Two points each.)

10. Two London killers who use the alias Robinson. (Two points each.)

11. Mirrors.
    a. a double reflection
    b. shattered with a hairbrush
    c. "I'll buy you a new mirror—it'll be your conscience."

Name the film for each mirror. (Two points each.)

12. Staircases. Which films contain staircases used in the following fashion? (Two points each.)
    a. Descending inappropriately dressed for the ball.
    b. Confronting a dog.
    c. Shot with his own gun.
    d. Suspicious milking.
    e. An inauspicious look over the railing.
    f. Heart aflutter.
    g. Shish-kebobing brother.
    h. Rapping with mom.
    i. Murdered by Mother.
    j. Tripped up by Uncle.
    k. Eyeing a diamond.

13. Itineraries. Identify the film by the following. (Two points each.)
    a. NYC; London; Amsterdam; London; Atlantic Ocean; London.
    b. (Moscow); Copenhagen, D.C.; NYC; D.C.; Cuba, D.C.; Paris.
    c. NYC; LI; NYC; IL; Hwy. 41; IL; SD.
    d. Somewhere, CA; Spring Valley; Soda City; NYC.
    e. Norway; Copenhagen; Berlin; Leipzig; Berlin; Sweden.

14. Supply the missing characters' names. (One point per name.)

I Confess O. E. Hasse (a) _____
             Dolly Haas (b) _____

Saboteur   Otto Kruger (c) _____
             Alma Kruger (d) _____

Extra Credit

15. What were the two French Resistance films Hitchcock directed? (Two points each.)

16. What was Dr. Goebbels's favorite Hitchcock picture? (Two points.)

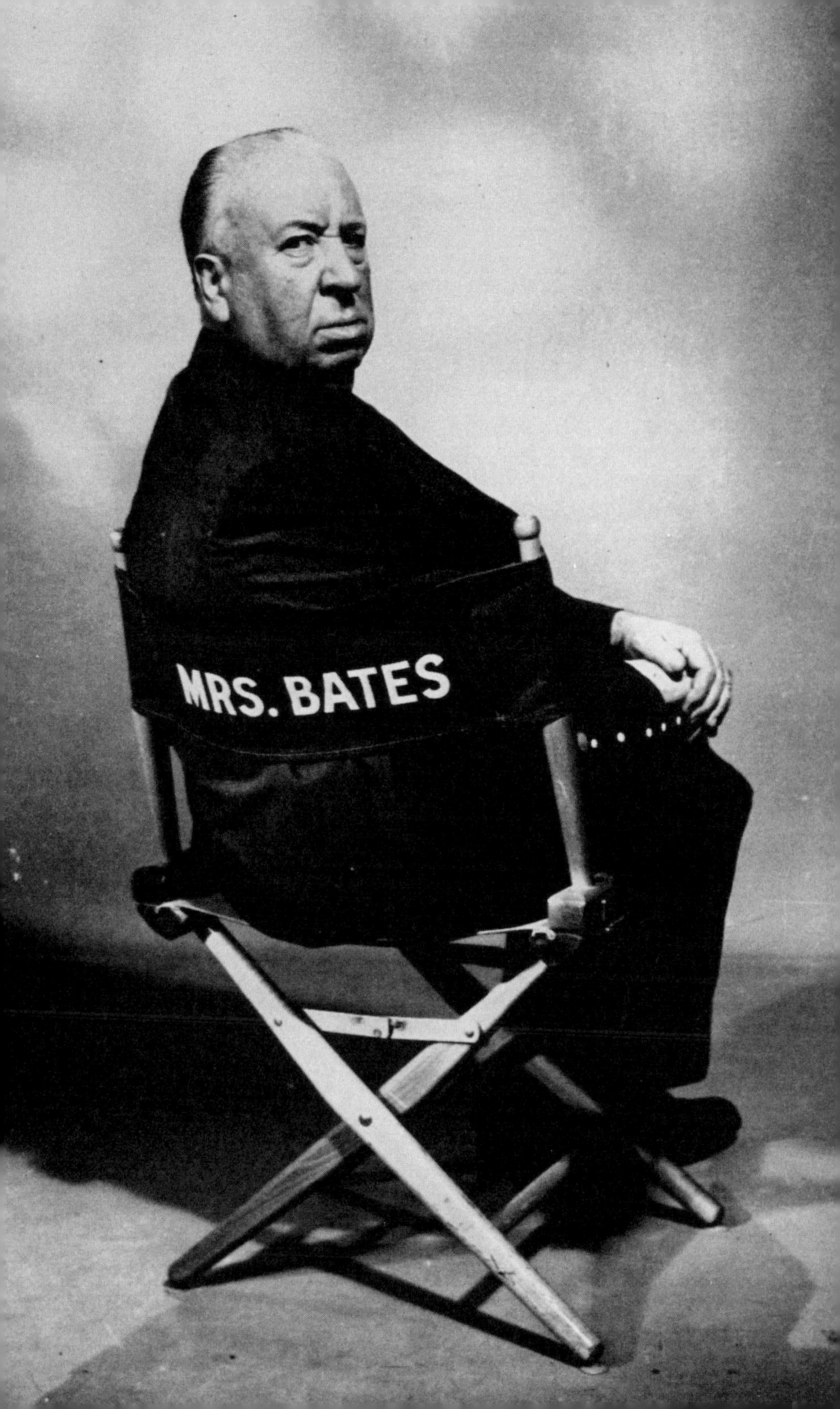
MRS. BATES

ANSWERS

BEGINNINGS

1. *Easy Virtue.*

2. *Rich and Strange.*

3. *Juno and the Paycock.*

4. *Downhill.*

5. *The Pleasure Garden.*

6. *The Ring.*

7. *The Manxman.*

8. *Champagne.*

9. *The Mountain Eagle.*

10. *The Farmer's Wife.*

11. *Waltzes From Vienna.*

12. *The Skin Game.*

13. *Number Seventeen.*

14. *The Mountain Eagle.* The six frames reproduced in the Truffaut book are probably all that remains.

15. A music hall. Very Weimar Republic, this music hall. Appropriately, much of this film was shot in Munich.

16. *The Ring.*

17. *Juno and the Paycock.*

18. *Easy Virtue.*

19. *The Skin Game.*

20. *Waltzes From Vienna.*

21. *The Manxman.*

22. *Elstree Calling.*

23. *Lord Camber's Ladies.*

THE LODGER

1. The Avenger.

2. Golden curls. Like Daisy's, as a matter of fact.

3. Tuesday.

4. Fashion model.

5. *The Evening Standard*.

6. To avenge his sister's death at the hands of the Avenger. His mother swore him to this task on her deathbed.

7. The sister's coming-out ball, at which siblings were dancing when the lights were doused and the murder was committed.

8. A dress that Daisy modeled at work.

9. Daisy. One of Joe's crude marriage jokes, the poor lunk, after he says, "When I've put a rope around the Avenger's neck, I'll put a ring around Daisy's finger."

10. A gun, newspaper clippings about the Avenger, a map charting his recent strikes and a photo of the departed sister.

11. Two weeks, beginning and ending on Tuesdays.

12. Hitchcock claimed he would have preferred for the Lodger to have gone walking off enigmatically into the fog, leaving the viewer uncertain as to whether or not he was the murderer. This was effectively scotched by the casting of matinee idol Ivor Novello as the title character. The studio was purportedly leery of ruining Novello's image with his fans.

13. Ivor Montagu. Montagu was evidently knocked out by the film, but suggested two improvements: cutting way down on the number of title frames (and having the remaining ones designed more elaborately) and reshooting some of the poorly lighted chase scenes at the end of the film.

BLACKMAIL

1. Going to the movies. Frank wants to go see *Fingerprints;* Alice keeps changing her mind, although it's clear from the beginning she's not going.

2. No. She takes a note out of her purse, obviously from the artist, saying that he will be there that night.

3. A laughing clown that points at the viewer. Alice, for whom the mockery hits too close to home, rips the canvas after the murder.

4. One of Alice's gloves.

5. Alice's other glove.

6. He tries to borrow money from the artist. Apparently he had been attempting to do it for a while, because he had left a number of messages for the artist at his apartment.

7. She imagines a cocktail shaker, which moves up and down in the sign, turning into a knife.

8. The artist's landlady. She gives a description of him to the police, he being naturally suspect since he had been hanging around a lot.

9. The British Museum.

10. The inspector, Frank's boss, gets a phone call just as Alice is about to confess, and, pressed for time, he asks Frank to handle Alice. Frank takes charge, and that's the end of that.

11. Tuesday. The artist's note to Alice says, "I'll be there on Tuesday. Will you?"

12. Tracy.

13. Joan Barry did the dialogue, standing off screen to say the lines (there was no dubbing at this stage) as Anny pantomimed. Ondra's Czech accent was judged to be too strong for English ears to understand. This accounts for the extravagant windups Ondra would do with her mouth every time she uttered a syllable, and probably also for the excessive amount of giggling done in this movie.

MURDER!

1. The three are in the same theater troupe. The murderer is in love with the accused; some sources list them as engaged.

2. Diana's defense is amnesia; she doesn't deny it so much as she says she doesn't remember, and her worthless counsel says she is not responsible for her actions during a swoon. Edna was killed by Handell Fane because she was revealing the man's dark secret: he was a half-caste. As it happened, Diana already knew.

3. Fane was dressed up in a policeman's outfit. Diana didn't hear him come in because she had her fingers in her ears, trying not to hear Edna's half-caste rap.

4. Diana had auditioned for his acting company about a year previously; he had sent her away to get some experience "in the provinces." Sir John finds a framed picture of himself in Diana's bedroom.

5. Sir John remembers the glass of brandy that was emptied at the scene

of the crime. It occurs to him, while shaving in front of his orchestra, that whoever drank that brandy committed the murder.

6. A cigarette case left behind in Fane's dressing room has a trace of dried blood; Diana identifies the case as Fane's. The clue in the dressing room is the broken sink directly under the window. It would appear that someone had to use the sink to get in or out of the window, which opens onto the alley that leads to Diana's place. That was the route taken by Fane the night of the murder.

7. Three. Nine vote guilty.

8. Sir John kind of offers Markham the job of stage manager in his next production, and hints around that he might have a plum role or something for his actress wife.

9. The cheese, as Sir John explains, is a big role in the new "play," the kind of role an actor would be nuts for. Fane is certain he's being set up when it turns out there's only one page to the entire script, and it ends smack-dab in the middle of the phrase "half-caste." Sir John's claim that he is looking for a "collaborator" doesn't quite cut it, and Fane leaves without exposing himself.

10. a) The suggestion is offered by Diana's landlady that for someone to be able to swarm up into Diana's room from the alley and through a small window, that person would have to be "an acrobat"—which, as it happens, Fane was before becoming an actor.
    b) Fane escapes the clutches of the law by hanging himself spectacularly from the high wire during his newly revived tightrope act. A confession has been conveniently left behind in his room.

11. One-thirty A.M.

12. Beethoven's Fifth Symphony, first movement, and the Overture from Wagner's *Tristan und Isolde*, respectively.

13. Mrs. Meachem.

14. *Mary*.

THE MAN WHO KNEW TOO MUCH

1. 1934: Sharpshooter. 1956: Singer.

2. 1934: St. Moritz. 1956: Marrakech.

3. 1934: London. 1956: Indianapolis, Indiana.

4. 1934: Betty. 1956: Hank.

5. 1934: Tabernacle of the Sun. 1956: Ambrose Chapel.

6. 1934: Shot in the back. 1956: Knife in the back.

7. 1934: Shot by Jill Lawrence. 1956: Falls to his death in Albert Hall during a struggle with Ben McKenna.

8. 1934: Shot by police. 1956: Shot with his own gun, again in a struggle with Ben.

9. 1934: Bob Lawrence sees Albert Hall tickets in assassin Ramon Levine's coat pocket, and Clive, after his escape, calls Jill, who goes there in an effort to stop the assassination. 1956: Jo goes there to find Inspector Buchanan when Ben is trapped inside Ambrose Chapel— having no idea about the assassination at first.

10. Rien, the 1956 assassin, gets a peek at a score, thoughtfully provided by his companion at the concert—although there is no indication that he can read one (or anything else for that matter).

11. Clive, the Lawrences' friend who graciously accompanies Bob on his sleuthing. He gets a good tooth yanked out, is hypnotized by an anarchist and gets thrown into jail for his pains.

12. Elizabeth Drayton, a greatly fleshed out and surprisingly sympathetic version of Peter Lorre's female accomplice.

13. The French inspector in Marrakech tells the McKennas that Louis Bernard was an agent for the FBI (or perhaps its British or Moroccan equivalent).

14. Hank proposed Louis Bernard for the bothersome task of removing snails from the McKenna backyard on hearing of Bernard's exotic culinary habits. "We tried everything to get rid of them," he says. "I never thought of a Frenchman." What cards, those Americans.

15. The second song Jo sings at the embassy, after the egregious "Whatever Will Be, Will Be (Que Será, Será)."

16. Drayton's sermon topic when the McKennas take in a service at Ambrose Chapel.

17. The address appears on the piece of paper in Louis Bernard's shaving brush.

18. Again, on the piece of paper in Bernard's shaving brush.

19. The various sufferings of Ben's patients. Ben and Jo make a whimsical list of ailments and services purchased that goes like this: Mrs. Camp-

bell's gallstones—the three days in Marrakech; Bill Edwards's tonsils—Jo's new dress; Johnny Matthews's appendix—Ben's suit; a multiplicity of delivered babies and Mrs. Morgan's hives—the boat trip over; Herbie Taylor's ulcers and Alida Markle's asthma—the trip home.

20. "I buy . . . and I sell," Bernard says to Jo, and then, to her irritated request for amplification, "Whatever makes the greatest profit."

21. Taking up the collection, the pivotal point certainly to many worship services.

22. He is the prime minister of an unnamed country. The country is kept deliberately vague; there is even a brief shot of the outside of the embassy, the identity of which is effectively obliterated for these purposes of deliberate vagueness.

23. The ambassador to England of the same unnamed country as the prime minister.

24. Bernard Herrmann, as the orchestra conductor.

25. "The Storm Cloud Cantata," by Arthur Benjamin.

26. A case of mistaken identity. Bernard is on the lookout for a foreign couple who have come to Morocco to arrange for an assassin. Bernard suspects the McKennas of being that couple, but it turns out to be the Draytons.

27. David Selznick.

28. The British Board of Film Censors was worried about the implication of policemen shooting off guns, something the police don't do in England. In the final shoot-out with the anarchists, the censors insisted that the army should tote the rifles, but the scene is fudged so that it is unclear who is actually doing the shooting. The incident was apparently modeled on a real shoot-out with a group of anarchists lead by a character named Peter the Painter (the model for Peter Lorre's character) in 1911. Winston Churchill, as home secretary, was the man who decided to send in the army.

29. It obviously doesn't matter at this point, but the date on the note in the shaving brush next to the notation "A. Hall" is March 21. The tickets for the concert that Levine takes in read March 22.

THE 39 STEPS

1. "How far is Winnipeg from Montreal?"

2. "Whoever pays the best." At the moment she is working for England.

3. The right hand. Ms. Smith misinforms Hannay on this point.

4. Hannay makes off with the farmer's overcoat after his escape. It is the inadvertent presence of a hymn book in the coat's pocket that saves Hannay's life, as the little book takes the bullet that Professor Jordan shoots at our hero. (And that is a hymn book, mind you, not a Bible.)

5. Once on the train out of London, where Hannay begs her indulgence in a little story and she will have none of it. (Eva Marie Saint, you will remember, proves more amenable in *North by Northwest* in the same situation.) Then again during the political rally, where Hannay is making a great impromptu talk, she spies him and feels it her civic duty to turn him in. The fact that she nearly gets killed by Jordan's henchmen for her incessant do-goodisms seems appropriate somehow.

6. After wrenching her hand out of the cuff and slipping away from the sleeping Hannay at the hotel, she is about to call out to the two men in the lobby she *still* thinks are policemen, when she hears them talking (it would appear to the professor's wife) about the 39 Steps. Only after finally discovering that Jordan's thugs are not cops (and that they plan to kill *her* as well) does she realize Hannay is telling the truth.

7. The tune is Mr. Memory's theme. Mr. Memory of course turns out to be the key to everything.

8. At the inn Pamela hears the thugs speak of it as Jordan's next destination. "He's picking up our friend at the London Palladium on the way out," they say. Then she tells Hannay and they leave for London.

9. Fifty. "The 39 Steps is an organization of spies, collecting information on behalf of the foreign office of . . ." (Transmission ends here.)

10. Specifications of English airplanes, which are presumably valuable to the unnamed but more-than-vaguely-Teutonic enemy. A secret vital to England's air defense, Ms. Smith says.

11. The town in Scotland where Jordan lives.

12. The name of the music hall revue at the London Palladium.

13. Joan Harrison.

14. The first scene shot was the one in which the handcuffed couple escaped from the thugs' car after the road was blocked by sheep. Appar-

ently within a short time of introducing Madeleine Carroll and Robert Donat, Hitchcock summarily handcuffed them together, then abruptly disappeared for more than several hours, conveniently mislaying the key.

SECRET AGENT

1. 1916. May 10, to be exact.

2. Edgar Brodie, novelist.

3. The government was of the opinion that he was too famous to be of any espionage use to them. And of course a novelist is the most logical choice to go off eliminating German spies. . . .

4. R.

5. To Arabia via Constantinople, to somehow undermine British war efforts.

6. The General is the hit man. "A lady killer, eh?" Ashenden says to R, who replies, "Not just ladies."

7. The friendly organist/agent who was throttled by the German spy managed to tear off one of the German's coat buttons during the struggle. As it happens, our agents discover Mr. Caypor is missing a button of exactly the same kind! Irrefutable evidence—this, plus the fact that his wife is German.

8. The first scene takes place during the roulette game in which the connection is made between buttons; as soon as Ashenden and the General exchange knowing looks, the dog rushes in alarm to his master. The more famous scene is the actual murder scene, in which the dog becomes increasingly more frantic as Mr. Caypor nears his end.

9. In a chocolate factory.

10. After the General and Ashenden have pulled the alarm in the chocolate factory, they are passed a note by a friendly operative that tells them of Marvin's perfidy.

11. The first is wrapped around a bar of chocolate and says that Edgar Brodie is alive and bothersome, and is staying at the Hotel Excelsior. The second gets passed along the conveyor belt at the chocolate factory and suggests that the police be anonymously informed of the presence of the two English spies.

12. It was a postcard, apparently for R's benefit, reading, "Home safely, but never again. Mr. and Mrs. Ashenden."

13. She is worried that such an act would poison a relationship with Ash-enden. "What do I care about our forces, or him?" she says. "It's us; I'm not going to have this on our consciences."

14. He was a morphine addict, and reportedly disappeared from the set continually to satisfy his habit.

SABOTAGE

1. Saturday is the Lord Mayor's Show Day.

2. Verloc puts sand in the electricity generators.

3. Because no one was frightened and the city was not thrown into chaos. LONDON LAUGHS AT BLACK-OUT, say the newspaper headlines, but the senior saboteurs are not amused. "We are not comedians," the superior says soberly.

4. The Bijou Cinema.

5. While spying on a group discussion between Verloc and his cohorts backstage at the cinema he is caught eavesdropping. One of the conspirators recognizes him.

6. That her bird won't sing.

7. A bird cage.

8. "Don't forget, the birds will sing at 1:45."

9. Verloc sends Stevie to a cloakroom at Piccadilly Circus. The bus driver nearly stops Stevie from getting on, saying that he is not allowed to carry flammable film. "Don't set fire to me or the other passengers," he says pleasantly.

10. The saboteurs, Verloc's buddies, conveniently blow up the cinema, and love interest Detective Sergeant Ted Spenser walks off with the guilty Mrs. V. One cop says to another, "She said her husband was dead before the bombing. Or was it after? I can't remember." Case closed.

11. *Bartholomew the Strangler*.

12. *Who Killed Cock Robin?*

YOUNG AND INNOCENT

1. A very jealous husband with a quite noticeable nervous affliction accuses his wife of fooling about with "boys."

2. Robert is a screenwriter, Christine is an actress, and they had been working together on a story idea that he had written. It stands to reason that Robert was the "boy" the murderer had seen hanging around.

3. First, he is seen running from the body on the beach by two girls. Secondly, it happens that the victim has left him money in her will.

4. It appears the belt from his raincoat was the murder weapon. (Damned sophisticated, those Scotland Yard forensics.)

5. Tom's Hat was the pub where Robert had left his raincoat behind.

6. Old Will, Erica hears from one of the Tom's Hat regulars, was in possession of the raincoat. Later on, he becomes the only one able to recognize the likely murderer, since the murderer gave him the coat.

7. The China Mender. Robert breaks a cup in the shelter in an effort to summon Old Will.

8. He swipes one of the statuettes already on the family's lawn and presents it as if it were a match to their existing set.

9. At court he swipes the eyeglasses of his nearly blind (and worthless) lawyer and slips away in this ingenious disguise. At Erica's aunt's house, he and Erica are only able to leave when the nosy woman is made "it" in the children's game of blindman's buff.

10. A matchbox in the pocket of the raincoat carries the name Grand Hotel. It turns out to be the hotel where our murderer is employed as house drummer.

11. Nobby's Lodging House.

12. The song is about "the drummer man," appropriately.

13. *The Girl Was Young*.

14. The murderer has probably framed Robert for the murder. For him to have had the belt to kill his wife, he would have had to steal the coat ahead of time. Whether he followed Robert to Tom's Hat or happened across him accidentally—or even stole the coat without realizing who Robert was—doesn't matter in this question of premeditation.

THE LADY VANISHES

1. She is smuggling a secret clause of a peace treaty out of the country, encoded somehow in a tune.

2. A minstrel of a sort who stands outside Miss Froy's window with his guitar and sings the tune that Miss Froy is to memorize.

3. He is a musicologist. Interesting that he can't remember the tune when Miss Froy teaches it to him later.

4. Someone drops a flower pot out of a window. The pot is meant for Miss Froy but ends up conking Iris on the head.

5. It is the tea bag Gilbert sees on the window. Miss Froy only drinks one brand of tea, and brings it with her because nobody else carries it. Iris remembers about the tea, the label of which appears briefly at the window while the garbage is being thrown out up ahead.

6. He has a vanishing lady trick.

7. Her high heels. (This is pre–Vatican II, remember.)

8. Besides palling at the prospect of blooshed she finds out Miss Froy is English, and is evidently stung by an abrupt surge of nationalism.

9. Mr. Todhunter, the hypocritical barrister on board with his mistress. Todhunter is our Isolationist, who, when attempting to appease the allegorical Fascists with a white flag, is summarily shot dead by his erstwhile allies.

10. You'll remember that Iris is going back to England to be married. Not a matter of passion, it would appear, because after her adventures with Gilbert, she avoids her conservative-looking fiancé at the station, and disappears with Gilbert.

11. Caldicott and Charters.

12. Hitchcock was assigned the script, written by Sydney Gilliatt and Frank Launder a couple of years earlier for another director, by producer Edward Black. Hitchcock purportedly shot it pretty much unchanged. This differed sharply from his usual intimate involvement with adapting the scenario.

JAMAICA INN

1. Nancy.

PHOTO QUIZ I: FUNNY PAPERS

1. Uncle Charlie is building a paper house for his niece, Ann, in *Shadow of a Doubt*.

2. The piece contains a story headlined WHERE IS THE MERRY WIDOW KILLER? This man turns out to be Uncle Charlie.

3. Niece Charlie goes to the library the following evening, where she reads the offending story.

4. Annabella Smith is holding a map of Scotland in *The 39 Steps*.

5. She has circled a town, Alt-na Shellach, where as it happens lives Professor Jordan, the head of the 39 Steps.

6. They are blackmail notes in *Dial M for Murder*.

7. Tony Wendice, Margot's husband.

8. An evidently interesting love note written by Mark here to Margot, which the blackmailer has stolen.

9. He is photographing a treaty between Cuba and the USSR, in *Topaz*.

10. Señor Rico Parra.

THE GREAT APPEARANCES QUIZ

1. q	7. m	13. c
2. n	8. k	14. j
3. f	9. p	15. h
4. a	10. e	16. g
5. l	11. b	17. o
6. i	12. d	18. *The Wrong Man*.

19. The newsroom appearance in *The Lodger*. He also later appeared in the crowd scene in which the Lodger is mobbed.

20. That would have to be *Dial M for Murder*. Technically, every time the camera picks up the reunion photo, Hitchcock is making his appearance. It's a trick question.

21. Hitchcock was originally to be floating down the Thames at the beginning of the film. The shot was only used in the film's trailer, however.

QUOTES QUIZ I

1. *Dial M for Murder*, Tony Wendice (Ray Milland).

2. *Vertigo*, Judy Barton (Kim Novak).

3. *Shadow of a Doubt*, Uncle Charlie Oakley (Joseph Cotten).

4. *Psycho*, Norman Bates (Anthony Perkins).

5. *North by Northwest*, a note from Roger Thornhill (Cary Grant), in his matchbook, to Eve (Eva Marie Saint).

6. *Rope*, Brandon Shaw (John Dall) and Philip (Farley Granger).

7. *Strangers on a Train*, Bruno Anthony (Robert Walker).

8. *Suspicion*, John Aysgarth (Cary Grant).

9. *To Catch a Thief*, Frances Stevens (Grace Kelly).

10. *The 39 Steps*, Richard Hannay (Robert Donat).

11. *Notorious*, Alicia Huberman (Ingrid Bergman).

12. *Stage Fright*, Charlotte Inwood (Marlene Dietrich).

13. *The Birds*, Mitch Brenner (Rod Taylor).

14. *Lifeboat*, Gus Smith (William Bendix).

15. *The Lady Vanishes*, Dr. Hartz (Paul Lukas).

16. *Mr. and Mrs. Smith*, David Smith (Robert Montgomery).

17. *Rear Window*, Lisa Fremont (Grace Kelly).

18. *Marnie*, Marnie Edgar (Tippi Hedren).

19. *Rebecca*, Mrs. Danvers (Judith Anderson).

20. *Spellbound*, Dr. Alex Brulov (Michael Chekov).

REBECCA

1. She is never given a first name, either in the novel or the movie. (Hitchcock named her Daphne, somewhat sarcastically one would think, during drafts of the screenplay.)

2. Rebecca is believed by most to have drowned in a boating accident. Maxim identified a body as hers—and we never do find out whose body it actually was. She really died in a struggle with Maxim, a domestic argument that so gets under the man's skin that he slaps her and she falls, hitting her head on some ship's tackle.

3. Favell is Rebecca's cousin. He had had a long-standing affair with Rebecca, and we eventually find out that Rebecca had been taunting Maxim during their final confrontation with the suggestion that she was going to have Favell's baby.

4. She breaks a figurine in Rebecca's old study, and stuffs the broken

pieces in a drawer. Later one of the servants is accused of making off with the thing, and the man is forced to protest his innocence.

5. Mrs. Danvers suggests that Mrs. de Winter wear a costume similar to one in one of the great ancestral portraits lining the hallway. She does not tell Mrs. de Winter that Rebecca wore the same dress to her last ball, knowing that this duplication will get a rise out of Maxim—which it does. When Mrs. de Winter figures out what must have happened, she confronts Mrs. Danvers in Rebecca's bedroom, whereupon the old woman suggests to the bride that she will never fill her former mistress's shoes, and that it would be an auspicious turn of events for all considered if Mrs. de Winter were to throw herself out of the window onto the rocks below.

6. Mrs. van Hopper. Mrs. de Winter's former employer, a social-climbing American matron vacationing clamorously in Monte Carlo.

7. Rebecca's dog. (To his credit, he does seem to make peace with the new wife.)

8. The manufacturers of Rebecca's underwear.

9. Old Ben, who says, "She's in the sea, you know?" to anyone handy.

10. Favell expects the doctor to say that Rebecca was pregnant, thereby assigning a motive of outraged jealousy to Maxim's alleged murder of his wife. What the doctor says is that Rebecca had cancer, which allows everyone to believe that she had committed suicide by drowning herself—conveniently overlooking Maxim's guilty face.

11. False. She did win for *Suspicion* a year later.

12. In the novel, Maxim confessed to his bride that he had shot Rebecca, and felt quite guiltless about it to boot. This would not do at all for the diligent Hays Office, which could not very well have a romantic leading man go committing a major crime and then waltz off into the sunset with his new bride, completely unsullied. The cause of death was changed to indicate an accident.

13. Manderley, the estate, which is treated as almost a breathing organism, infused as it is with the presence of Rebecca.

FOREIGN CORRESPONDENT

1. The New York *Morning Globe*.

2. Huntley Haverstock.

3. The Universal Peace Party.

4. Three. His nephew steals one, he leaves one in Van Meer's cab, and one gets blown into water at the windmill.

5. Van Meer is a Dutch diplomat who knows the secret clause (Clause 27, as it happens) in a peace treaty between Holland and Belgium. Of course we never find out what's in the clause; it is our MacGuffin for the evening.

6. One, presumably the Belgian diplomat of corresponding rank.

7. Amsterdam.

8. To signal an okay to landing planes.

9. a. Krug.
   b. Rowley.

10. ffolliott means for Fisher to think that his daughter, Carol, has been kidnapped in order to force him into revealing where he is holding Van Meer. In truth, Johnny Jones is staying with her out of town—she thinks she is helping to keep him safe—but when she hears him booking an extra room for her at the hotel, she bolts in a what-kind-of-girl-do-you-think-I-am huff back to Daddy's house, walking in just as the old man is about to spill the beans.

11. The final scene in London where Johnny broadcasts Edward R. Murrow—style back to America while the Germans blitz vociferously.

MR. AND MRS. SMITH

1. Ann Smith's maiden name.

2. The man from Ann's hometown who brings the news about their illegal marriage.

3. David's club, where he sleeps when kicked out of his apartment.

4. The club where Chuck Benson and David double-date, and at which Jeff and Ann show up.

5. The intimate restaurant David and Ann frequented in more passionate days, which has since become a dive.

6. David and Jeff's law firm.

7. David and Ann had planned to vacation there before the blowup; Jeff

and Ann travel there to meet the former's parents, and David shows up anyway.

8. Ann's hometown.

9. Ann asks, "If you had it to do all over again, would you marry me?" David answers truthfully.

10. There was a border dispute between Idaho and Nevada, and although the Smiths thought they had a license from the proper state, they were actually in the wrong state.

11. Knowing of the much-reported comment of Hitchcock's that actors were cattle, she arranged for a corral to appear on the set, replete with three noisy heifers that bore name tags identifying them as herself, Robert Montgomery and Gene Raymond.

SUSPICION

1. The book Lina is reading on the train when she first meets Johnny.

2. The party Johnny crashes, secreting Lina away and subsequently proposing.

3. The cliff-side property Johnny proposes as the site for his (and Beaky's) big real estate deal.

4. A pair of chairs, apparently of great ancestral value, which Johnny eventually pawns.

5. His portrait.

6. He is fired after an unexpected audit finds him £2000 short. Mahlbeck accuses him of stealing the money.

7. Beaky dies drinking a beaker of brandy on a bet in a bar in Paris. Lina seems convinced of Johnny's guilt, first of all because Johnny and Beaky's corporation had not yet been dissolved (meaning Johnny stood to walk away with a lot of money from the business), and secondly because bystanders reported that an Englishman needled Beaky into drinking the brandy.

8. Johnny is in Liverpool trying to borrow on Lina's insurance.

9. *The Trial of Richard Palmer*. It is significant because the villain of the book kills someone by inducing him to drink brandy.

10. An untraceable poison. Isabel was informed of this by her brother, the coroner (who is appropriately adept at carving his Cornish hen).

11. These were two ways to end the Mahlbeck affair, the first a way to pay Mahlbeck back, the second a preparation for suicide when the first did not work.

12. Hitchcock always claimed the studio prevented him from this ending: Lina can't bear to live without Johnny, so she purposely drinks the poisoned milk. At the same time, she writes a letter to her mother explaining the situation, seals it and gives it to Johnny to mail—which he does, cheerfully popping it in the mailbox while Lina breathes her last. Another of those many stories from his own apocrypha that Hitchcock told repeatedly. (Apparently the novel from which the film is taken, *Before the Fact* by Francis Iles, does have the Lina character murdered by the husband.)

SABOTEUR

1. First, the fire set in the defense plant at the beginning of the film. Second, the match held to the automatic fire alarm/extinguisher Barry used to escape from the storage room. Third, Barry manages to prevent the explosion of a new battleship at the Brooklyn Navy Yard (even though he is not so successful with the dedication party).

2. He has unknowingly handed his friend, Tony, a fire extinguisher filled with gasoline at the site of the defense plant fire.

3. Pat Martin is a model whom Barry sees repeatedly on billboards before meeting her in the flesh.

4. The letter that Fry drops at the plant carries this address. It is Barry's first clue in chasing the man.

5. He reads this address on the telegram sent by Fry to Spring Valley.

6. Fry is sitting in the back of a truck at the Brooklyn Navy Yard, preparing to blow up the battleship that is being dedicated.

7. On the fan of a car.

8. The General.

9. Charles Tobin and Mrs. Van Sutton.

10. He holds an impromptu charity auction with Mrs. Van Sutton's jewelry.

11. Joan Harrison, who left Hitchcock to go out on her own after this film, and Norman Lloyd, who played Fry.

12. At one point Fry, riding in a taxi, smirks at the sight of a battleship on its side. The implication is that he (or a colleague) was responsible for the condition of the ship. As it happened, Hitchcock inserted actual newsreel footage of the French ship *Normandie*, which had been converted into the *USS Lafayette* and subsequently capsized in a mysterious fire in New York Harbor. The Navy thought this implication of sabotage a slur on its vigilance.

13. Dorothy Parker.

SHADOW OF A DOUBT

1. The first is obviously the fact that Charlie has decided to cable her uncle exactly as Uncle Charlie is cabling his arrival. The second instance has to do with the theme from "The Merry Widow Waltz," which Charlie cannot get out of her head at the dinner table that first night; there is no explanation for its presence there except that it had already been present in Uncle Charlie's mind.

2. St. Paul, Minnesota. Forty-six Birnham Street.

3. Charles throws his hat on Charlie's bed.

4. To Ann a stuffed animal, to Roger a pistol and holster, to Joe a wristwatch, to Emma a fur coat and framed pictures of their parents.

5. "He's in business . . . the way men are."

6. TS FROM BM.

7. Thelma Schenley (Mrs. Bruce Matthewson), one of the Merry Widow Killer's victims. We read this in the newspaper in the library—it was the story that Uncle Charlie had torn out of the paper.

8. a. Charlie gives it back to Charles in the bar, after he has pretty much admitted that he is a killer. b. Charlie wears it again during the reception after Charles's speech to the ladies' club, in an attempt to force him to leave town.

9. Three. We read this in the newspaper story as well.

10. Charles was riding a bicycle on an icy road and ran into a streetcar. Emma professes that he was never the same afterward—it is the closest to a rational explanation for Uncle Charlie's psychopathy that we will get.

11. Jack takes her to Gunner's Grill (where they will presumably have a

grinder); Uncle Charlie takes her to the 'Til Two Bar (where he has two double brandies).

12. Thornton Wilder, whose *Our Town* Hitchcock had admired, and who understood well the small-town setting Hitchcock wanted to capture with fidelity.

13. Hitchcock's mother, Emma, died on September 26, 1942. Spoto, in *The Dark Side of Genius*, makes a fascinating case for the very personal nature of *Shadow of a Doubt* for Hitchcock. Among other things, Spoto asserts that the character of Emma Newton was modeled on Mrs. Hitchcock, whose death left the director with much sorrow and guilt.

LIFEBOAT

1. a. George Spencer, "Joe" to his friends.
    b. Kovac.
    c. Constance Porter.
    d. Stanley Garrett.
    e. Willy, the German.

2. 4–2 is the vote. Gus and Kovac issue the minority opinion against Willy. Joe abstains, apparently feeling disenfranchised, and poor doomed Mrs. Higgins, after railing at Willy for killing her baby, breaks down into incoherence.

3. Kovac's family is from Czechoslovakia. Gus's real last name is Schmidt.

4. She knows she is headed for the probable resumption of a doomed love affair with a married man, who is also stationed in England, so she is grateful for the change of course.

5. In order: her camera, mink coat, typewriter, suitcase and Cartier bracelet.

6. Willy takes charge when waves threaten to capsize the boat, calling out "Fools, save yourselves!"

7. Energy pills and food tablets.

8. Even more than the fact that he has just killed Gus, the revelation that he has had a flask of water all this time is particularly galling. His sweat gives him away.

9. Kovac plans to buy one of Rittenhouse's factories and turn it into the "workers' paradise."

10. The camera goes underwater to peek at a comatose-looking fish nuzzling Connie's Cartier.

11. The weight reduction system advertised on the back of a paper Gus reads near the beginning of the film, under which title Hitchcock makes his ritual cameo. As it happened, Hitchcock had been under a strict diet which resulted in him shrinking (if one could call it that) from 300 to 200 pounds, and inserted before and after shots of himself in this phony ad for a fictitious product.

12. Al Magarulian was Gus's main rival in dancing the jitterbug and, more importantly, for Gus's girl, Rosie. There is some discussion of his negative qualities. It is also debated whether it was Al Magarulian or Kovac who introduced Rosie to Gus.

13. She took to wearing no underwear, a factor which apparently became clear when she climbed to the water tank each day where the film was shot.

14. Ernest Hemingway.

15. Ernest Hemingway.

SPELLBOUND

1. He has had a breakdown and has been labeled insufficiently healthy (and sane?) by the hospital's board.

2. Garmes thinks he is responsible for his father's death. Mary Carmichael has an extreme hatred of men.

3. *The Labyrinth of the Guilt Complex.*

4. These to choose from: the fork lines in the tablecloth; lines on Constance's robe; railroad tracks; the operating room; the whiteness of Dr. Brulov's bathroom; the lines on Brulov's quilt; sled marks outside the window at Brulov's house; the ski marks made as our protagonists ski.

5. Constance finds that the hospital's copy of Dr. Edwardes's book is autographed. The handwriting is quite different from that on a note the imposter sent to her earlier in the day.

6. At the beginning of the story Murchison claims he never knew Dr. Edwardes. But, after the trial, and when Murchison has been reinstated, he tells Constance he knew Edwardes only slightly. The "slightly" bounces around in her head for a while until she realizes what it means.

7. Poor John accidentally skewered his brother on the tip of an iron fence. He finally remembers as he and Constance are skiing down the same mountain Edwardes died on (the association was what made him black out and assume Edwardes's identity, you see), which is fortunate for all concerned, since Constance seems willing to carry their session (the first recorded back-projected psychoanalysis) right off the side of the mountain.

8. a. The revolver was the wheel that the hooded figure dropped.
   b. The steep roof he was standing on was the ski slope.

9. a. The 21 Club in New York.
   b. The ski resort was Gabriel Valley.

10. The hotel detective at the Empire State Hotel says this to Constance.

11. Dr. Fleurot.

12. Rohmer and Chabrol report that the film was to be half in color and half in black-and-white, according to the film's differing states of consciousness. As it turns out, there is one bit of color, a flash of red, at the very end when Murchison shoots himself (and the camera). Rohmer and Chabrol also say that the original idea of the film (which was taken from a novel, *The House of Dr. Edwardes,* by a pseudonymous Francis Beeding) involved a Murchison figure who conducted black masses and had the cross of Christ tattooed on the soles of his feet, so as to commit blasphemy with his every step.

13. Best score, which was written by Miklos Rozsa. Interestingly enough, Selznick originally suggested Bernard Herrmann for the task.

NOTORIOUS

1. Miami, 1946.

2. He is not given one.

3. Suicide by poison capsule.

4. Washington.

5. Mrs. Sebastian straightaway wants to know why Alicia did not testify at her father's trial.

6. Emile makes a fuss over a bottle the first night she has dinner at the Sebastians'.

7. Hupka is made to have an accident in his car. Alex mourns his passing because "he was a first-class metallurgist."

8. UNICA.

9. 1934.

10. Dr. Anderson begins to drink her coffee by mistake, and the protests from Alex and Mother clue her in to the situation.

11. Professor Renzler.

12. Captain Prescott.

13. Pan Am.

THE PARADINE CASE

1. Major Paradine is murdered by his wife, Maddalena.

2. Sir Simon Flaquer is the family solicitor, Anthony Keane the barrister.

3. Mrs. Paradine's lust for Andre Latour, her husband's groom.

4. A spiked glass of burgundy.

5. The headboard of Mrs. Paradine's bed contains a portrait of her.

6. Keane attempts to pin the rap on Latour, suggesting the murder was Latour's effort to possess his mistress. No one seems to believe this except the increasingly silly Mr. Keane, of course, and the defendant won't cooperate with her own defense.

7. Keane manages to find out that Major Paradine's beloved dog was once poisoned by Latour in an effort to put the beast out of its misery.

8. Latour's suicide, triggered by the groom's shame and Keane's neurotic questioning.

9. The judge makes a pass at Gay Keane, the barrister's wife. He later likens the human brain to a walnut, which he appropriately picks apart.

10. Judy is convinced that Keane is harboring improper sentiments toward his client. Her father sticks up for his colleague's professional standards.

11. Roast chicken, roast potatoes and cauliflower au gratin.

12. She begins smoking.

13. He had wanted to cast a coarser man—"a man who really reeked of manure"—to emphasize the animal aspect of Mrs. Paradine's attraction to him. The smooth Jourdan was purportedly pressed on Hitchcock by Selznick.

14. His hair was grayed. At one point there was apparently thought of having him grow a mustache, but a random sampling of photos of real London barristers produced nary a one.

PHOTO QUIZ II: PRECIOUS FAMILY TIES AND INTIMATE DISCUSSIONS

1. A slide of the flower garden in Jeff's apartment courtyard in *Rear Window*.

2. Jeff has noticed a striking difference in this and another slide of the same scene. One slide was taken several days before the other, and shows a flower in Lars Thorwald's garden standing taller than the second slide. The assumption is that something has been buried in the garden very recently—perhaps bits of Mrs. Thorwald.

3. Miss Froy, the vanished lady in *The Lady Vanishes*.

4. Dr. Hartz had planned to remove her from the train and perform a purposely fatal operation.

5. It is the little girl's birthday party in *Young and Innocent*.

6. Robert and Erica manage to get out only after her aunt has been blindfolded in a game of blindman's buff.

7. The coffee Alicia is going to be given is poisoned in *Notorious*.

8. Dr. Anderson, who is suggesting Alicia go with him to the mountains.

9. Mrs. Drayton is telling Hank to whistle as loud as he can—"harder than you ever have in your life" in the second version of *The Man Who Knew Too Much*. The idea is to attract attention so that the child will be rescued.

10. Hank's mother is singing "Whatever Will Be, Will Be," alias "Que Será, Será."

ROPE

1. Brandon mentions that Philip is going away to practice for an upcoming concert engagement and that he is giving some first edition books to Mr. Kentley. 2. Kenneth is Janet's former boyfriend. Brandon claims to be ignorant of the fact that they have split up. 3. Mr. Kentley takes exception to Rupert's droll recitation of events of justified homicide—to reduce the lines at restaurants, etc. 4. Brandon is convinced that Rupert could never

carry out his stated hypothesis that murder is a privilege for a few selected superior beings. Brandon feels that he has been bold enough to put into practice what Rupert can only hypothesize. 5. Apparently, Philip used to throttle chickens in his youth, not an unheard-of practice, but one, under the circumstances, that Philip vehemently denies. 6. The party eats cold chicken. 7. "These hands will make you famous," Mrs. Atwater says. 8. Brandon ties the rope around the first editions and gives them to Mr. Kentley. 9. There is a hat in the closet bearing the monogram DK. 10a. Rupert claims to have left his cigarette case behind. 10b. He has brought back the rope. 11. The second cut takes place during the discussion of Philip's chicken killing, and cuts from Philip to Rupert. 12. "Mouvement Perpétuel #1" by Francis Poulenc. 13. Mrs. Wilson. 14. Ten minutes, the total length of a reel of film in 1948.

UNDER CAPRICORN

1. Their groom. He taught Hattie how to ride.

2. Flusky offers Charles a chance to make a quick profit by buying some crown land (with borrowed money) and selling it to himself (Flusky) at a substantial profit. Sam was prohibited by law from buying any more land from the crown.

3. Seven years. The brother was going to shoot Hattie. Honor, you understand.

4. Sam is hoping that enough of the local wives will be curious to see the governor's cousin so that the dinner will be a success and Hattie will rise to the occasion.

5. He was the only Adare who was a bad horseman. He had lamed her favorite horse years ago, and his bad horsemanship would end up being a great deal of trouble later on.

6. She is giving Hattie enormous draughts of her sleeping medicine in an effort to poison her, and is provoking some additional hysteria with the use of a shrunken head she occasionally places in her mistress's bed.

7. She has the empty liquor bottles from Hattie's room dumped out in front of the kitchen help.

8. The ring of keys, which Charles had earlier insisted she take from Milly. (The keys to the house, and the politics of their possession, are significant as well to *Rebecca* and *Notorious*.) Hattie signals the change in the servants' treatment by throwing out the switch that Milly used to beat them with.

9. The accidental shooting of Charles by Sam, and the governor's subsequently stated purpose of having Sam sent up for a second crime.

10. Winter, whom we meet in the beginning when he becomes Flusky's secretary (whatever that means in Sam's case), has gotten a five-year sentence for being involved with a girl whose father objected—i.e., for "getting her in trouble."

11. Eighteen thirty-one.

12. Minyago Yugilla. "Why weepest thou?"

13. Ingrid Bergman met Roberto Rossellini during the filming of *Under Capricorn*.

STAGE FRIGHT

1. Jonathan tells Eve that Charlotte killed her husband, when in actuality it was Jonathan. "She goaded me into it," he later allows.

2. They are in the *set* of a carriage, possibly a hansom cab, in the back of the theater.

3. Charlotte's bloodstained dress.

4. Freddie Williams, her producer.

5. Smith's nickname is "Ordinary." His Christian name is Wilfred.

6. The maid's name is Nellie Goode. The name of the pretend maid is Doris Tinsdale.

7. None.

8. A happy marriage.

9. He successfully pleaded self-defense. Smith has neglected to point out this previous incident to the Gills.

10. Jonathan contends that the blood splashed onto the dress during the murder, yet it becomes clear that the majority of the stain was smeared on deliberately.

11. "La Vie en Rose" and "The Laziest Gal in Town," respectively.

12. Patricia Hitchcock, Alfred and Alma's daughter, was attending the Royal Academy of Dramatic Arts at the time, as is Eve Gill in the film. *Stage Fright* also marks Pat's first role in one of her father's films, in which she is dubbed with the unfortunate name Chubby Bannister.

STRANGERS ON A TRAIN

1. No. Hitchcock seems to indicate that the meeting was pure chance—or fate, if you will. It is even Guy's foot that accidentally knocks Bruno's under the table.

2. "I beg your pardon, aren't you Guy Haines?" is said first by Bruno, and at the end of the movie by a priest, causing Guy and Ann to bolt from the car, reasonably enough. "Excuse me," is the first line of the film, spoken by Guy.

3. Metcalf.

4. At a record shop.

5. A TO G, with crossed tennis rackets.

6. Yes. Bruno calls Guy while the latter is suiting up for his doubles match at Southampton.

7. Magic Isle.

8. The Capitol dome.

9. The tune the calliope is playing both during Miriam's murder and the final scene in the amusement park.

10. The college Professor Collins teaches at. Collins, you will recall, meets Guy on the train to Washington the night of the murder and is Guy's alibi until it is discovered that he was so drunk he couldn't remember Guy.

11. Hennessey is the cop assigned to keep an eye on Guy.

12. The name of the boat Bruno rides into the Tunnel of Love after Miriam and her two boyfriends. Also, not insignificantly, the Greek god of the underworld.

13. The subject of Mrs. Anthony's painting.

14. c, a, b, i, e, d, h, f, g.

15. Bruno's tie clip.

16. Barbara Morton. She and Miriam resemble one another, with their round, squeezable faces and throats, and similar glasses. Bruno obviously sees the similarity during their two meetings, at the tennis club and at the Mortons' party.

17. Miriam's glasses.

18. The first trip: a boy points a toy gun at Bruno, Bruno pops the kid's balloon with his cigarette.

19. The second trip: during the struggle on the carousel with Guy, a boy on a horse hits at Bruno. Bruno pushes him off the horse and the kid is almost killed.

20. Three. Miriam, Bruno and the carousel operator, whom the police kill while shooting at Guy.

21. A double bass.

22. Bruno is sent to an asylum and is last seen in a straitjacket.

23. Hammond.

I CONFESS

1. "I can't believe it. We're free." She says it in the flashback, too (though thoughtfully leaving Logan out of the pronoun).

2. None.

3. At 11:30; estimated by the amount of a meal he had digested. Ruth later testified that she had left Logan at 11:00. Villette was killed on a Tuesday night, which we find out the next day, Wednesday. Wednesday, as Keller points out, is the day he works in Villette's garden.

4. Four people. Villette, Alma, the cook that Keller shoots in the hotel kitchen and Keller himself.

5. "Forgive me."

6. Keller says that on the night of the murder *he* was in the church and *Logan* came in upset.

7. In his office he is shown balancing a coin between two forks over a glass of water. Later he is seen at the Grandforts' residence balancing a glass of water on his forehead. It may be significant that he spills some of the water on himself—a scales-of-justice joke.

8. Ruth has given the police a motive for Logan's alleged murder of Villette—the latter's blackmail. She thought she was giving Logan an alibi, saying he was with her until eleven o'clock; Larrue of course has not told her of the coroner's findings about the time of death.

9. Logan's parish is St. Marie's in Quebec.

10. Ruth last saw Logan five years before, during his ordination.

11. No. Logan denies that it was his, and Robertson just lets it drop. (Or perhaps Hitchcock just let it drop, preferring not to deal with it any longer.)

12. Keller expects to be killed momentarily, his loneliness to end. Logan, he says, is friendless, and because of the verdict (which implied an impurity of vocation and of faith more than it cleared Logan of the murder) is more alone than ever, and is condemned to stay that way. If the movie is partly about faith, then Keller rejects it and Logan, although struggling, accepts it, and appears to be vindicated in the end.

13. His Method acting. That, and the presence of his acting coach, Mira Rostova, to whom he would turn constantly for advice on the set.

14. Björk apparently arrived in Hollywood with an illegitimate child and lover, and Jack Warner (the picture was made for Warner Bros.) flipped out, the memories of Ingrid Bergman and Roberto Rossellini fresh in his mind.

DIAL M FOR MURDER

1. Money. Margot is apparently privy to some inherited cache of money, and Tony, who is under the impression that she plans to leave him and change her will (for which he is the current beneficiary), is worried that he will not be able to keep himself in the style to which he is accustomed.

2. Eleven o'clock.

3. Swan apparently lifted some proceeds from the college ball, for which he was honorary treasurer. "Poor old Alfred" was the fall guy.

4. There is the business of a Miss Wallace who, after being led along the garden path by Swan and somehow making her finances available to him, is subsequently drawn to an overdose of something or another. The police believe suicide, but Tony, who spied on the whole process, knows better.

5. Tony has been selling sports equipment. Mark is a mystery writer.

6. Tony had badgered Margot into completing a long-procrastinated task, putting the newspaper clippings from his tennis days into a scrapbook.

7. Tony thinks the blackmail notes he wrote "put the fear of God into them."

8. Margot's latchkey is under the fifth step stair carpet. Swan's is in Margot's purse, where Tony stuck it after retrieving it from Swan's coat, thinking it was Margot's.

9. Hubbard is notified that Tony is spending a large quantity of one-pound

notes around town, and he decides he must get a look at Tony's bank statement in order to determine why. To do so, he pinches what he thinks is Margot's latchkey from her purse at the prison—only he can't get into the apartment because, as we know from the previous question, the key is Swan's and not Margot's.

10. Ironically, Margot has decided to stay with Tony, which was the reason she stopped writing to Mark. "You don't understand," she says to Mark, "he's changed." He has indeed, the bastard.

11. Spaghetti.

12. 3-D. Reportedly it is a cumbersome business to film in 3-D, but the result is well worth seeing, if one is able to find a theater exhibiting it.

13. Captain Lesgate.

REAR WINDOW

1. a
2. d
3. g
4. f

5. e
6. b
7. c

8. "Here lie the broken bones of L. B. Jeffries.

9. Four.

10. The first.

11. Stella is a nurse for the insurance company.

12. The killing of the dog. Jeff and Lisa are convinced that Thorwald did it because the dog knows too much.

13. His wife's wedding ring. The theory is that she wouldn't have left without it—that a wife *never* takes off her wedding ring—and if it is still behind, it is proof that she is dead. They expect the ring to be in the purse on the bedpost. It is an oft-pointed-out (but still irresistible) irony that Lisa, in trying to prove herself to Jeff, expects to win a ring from him by stealing the dead wife's ring. It is also interesting to note that Jeff's earlier desire to be rid of Lisa is finally turned dramatically on its head now that it appears that Thorwald might come back and do it for him. (Isn't this educational?)

14. "What have you done with her?"

15. In the early morning hours of day three, Thorwald leaves his apartment

with a woman. It is important because, at this point, it is conceivable that it might be the still-breathing Mrs. Thorwald. Doyle reports later that several people saw them leave together.

16. His wife's clothes.

17. To her mother's. The postcard read, "Feeling better already."

18. Photographing an accident during an auto race. From the photos we see at the beginning, it appears as if he is standing in the middle of the track and a wheel from one of the cars is heading right for him.

19. After the killing of the dog, Jeff notices, while comparing a slide he had taken a short time ago of the garden with a current slide of the same subject, that a particular flower is shorter than it once was.

20. He assumes Jeff is out to blackmail him. "What do you want from me?" he asks Jeff in anguish.

21. In the East River. The head is in a hatbox, and was presumably what was once buried in the garden. We get this all secondhand from an arresting cop as they haul poor Thorwald away.

22. Ninth Street, 125 Ninth, to be exact. (Two extra points for exact address.)

23. Laura.

TO CATCH A THIEF

1. Robie was a trapeze artist traveling with an American circus; after the circus left him stranded, he put his acrobatic skill to a more lucrative purpose. Eventually he was caught and sent to prison, but the prison was bombed during the war. Robie escaped and joined the French Resistance, and was subsequently paroled after the war for his heroics.

2. First of all, it seems as if they are slightly resentful of his relatively affluent standard of living, while they slave away in Bertani's kitchen. Secondly, as former thieves with Robie, they resent having any suspicion thrown their way as a result of the Cat's renewed antics (but this is of course more complicated than it seems at first, since it happens that at least some of them are responsible for these new thefts).

3. Oil was struck on their seemingly barren little piece of property. Jessie's husband, Jeremiah, was "a small-time swindler" who died just before this happened.

4. Bertani. Lloyd's of London.

5. Bertani. Danielle Foussard, the daughter of one of Robie's old Resistance pals.

6. At the beach at Cannes, after Danielle helped him escape from the police at Bertani's. Robie was dropped offshore in a bathing suit and swam nonchalantly to the beach as if he were just a swimmer, but Frances spotted him.

7. The note reads, "Robie, you've already gambled 8 of your 9 lives. Don't use the last one up."

8. Foussard had a wooden leg, which would have made it impossible to perform the acrobatics the Cat executed.

9. The list is in his coat pocket when he changes and goes for a swim with Frances (and, inadvertently, Danielle); when he returns to dress, the sheet has the mark of a wet thumbprint.

10. He raises grapes and flowers.

11. Mr. Burns of Oregon. He is in lumber.

12. Art Buchwald.

THE TROUBLE WITH HARRY

1. Three.

2. Captain Wiles, shooting at rabbits. Miss Gravely, who was accosted by a rabid Harry and pulled into the bushes, hit him with the metal cleat of her hiking boot.

3. Harry first confronted Jennifer at her front door, apparently claiming his nuptial rights as legal husband—she had run away from him and apparently did not expect him to turn up—and she hit him with a milk bottle. He stumbled off into the woods, mumbling about the same nuptial rights, and eventually ventured upon Miss Gravely, obviously mistaking her for his wife. This was when Harry attempted to have his way with Miss Gravely and she was obliged to strike him for the second time.

4. "Harry the handsome hero, Harry the saint, Harry the good," as Jennifer says, married her after his brother, Robert, her *first* husband, had died. It was the honorable thing to do, of course. Harry did not show up on the wedding night after he read his horoscope in a magazine in the hotel lobby (he was a Taurus) that said, "Don't start any new projects today," as they couldn't be finished.

5. Jennifer, two boxes of fresh strawberries the first day of each month; Arnie, a chemical set; Wiggy, a cash register (chromium-plated, one that rings a bell); Captain Wiles, a shotgun, corduroy britches, plain shirt, brown hunting cap; Miss Gravely, a hope chest.

6. A double bed.

7. Harry's brown shoes, which a tramp picked off of the body, and the sketch Sam did of the deceased, which Sam leaves behind in Mrs. Wiggs's store.

8. Sam draws over and erases parts of his sketch in the presence of the horrified Wiggs, and Captain Wiles steals the shoes from Wiggs's truck.

9. Heart attack.

10. Harry does, actually. It is after the three gunshots; a voice says, rather faintly (in the distance), "Okay, I know how to handle your type." It is not clear at the time, but later, after Miss Gravely tells her harrowing tale, it becomes obvious that Harry was confronting the poor woman.

11. Highwater.

12. A frog and two blueberry muffins.

13. Bernard Herrmann.

THE WRONG MAN

1. Manny plays bass at the Stork Club.

2. To borrow on Rose's insurance policy when she discovers she needs three hundred dollars to get four impacted wisdom teeth extracted.

3. July 9 he and Rose were vacationing in Cornwall, New York. In December Manny had a bad tooth and a distinctly swollen jaw—which, they reason, the insurance clerks would not have been able to miss. As it was, the jaw played no part in their description.

4. Three. On that date Manny spent the entire day playing cards with a Mr. Lamarka, a Mr. Molinelli and a third man who was an ex–prize-fighter. The first two people, as it happens, are both dead, and no one can even remember the boxer's name.

5. To a liquor store and then a delicatessen that had been robbed recently, possibly by the same man. Apparently, none of these shop people can identify Manny.

6. The last phrase of the note reads, "Give me the money from the cash

drawer." Both the actual holdup note and the *second* note Manny prints make the mistake of saying "draw" for "drawer."

7. The DA says Manny needed the money to pay off his bookies.

8. One of the jurors stands up and says, "Your honor, do we have to sit here and listen to this?" A prejudicing presumption of guilt.

9. His rosary beads. He is praying "for strength," as his mother suggests.

10. "Do you realize what you've done to my wife?" (He doesn't say this, unfortunately, to the arresting cop who pats him on the shoulder and says, "Okay, Manny?")

11. Rose was in the asylum for two years. The family moved to Florida when she was released.

12. Their address was 4024 Seventy-eighth Street, Jackson Heights, Queens.

13. January 14, 1953.

VERTIGO

1. Midge did.

2. He married into it.

3. Elster claims Carlotta is Madeleine's great-grandmother. Carlotta lived from 1831 to 1857, as shown with some legibility on her headstone.

4. (a) Madeleine buys a posy like the one held by Carlotta in her portrait; (b) Mission Dolores—Carlotta's grave is here; (c) the California Legion of Honor—Carlotta's portrait is here; (d) the McKittrick Hotel was once the site of the Valdes home (or so Elster says).

5. Yes, once, as Madeleine pulls away from Scottie's house in her car, Scottie standing on the front porch.

6. The rich man who seduced the innocent young Carlotta took the child that she bore and "threw her away." Afterward she went walking about, asking total strangers if they had seen her child. "A man could do that in those days," Pop Liebel says. "They had the power and the freedom." That phrase—"power and freedom"—is used quite prominently in the film, by Elster wistfully remembering the old San Francisco, and bitterly by Scottie in his final scene with Judy.

7. "Where is my child?"

8. "Wandering."

9. Coit Tower.

10. Scottie insists on it, in order to make Madeleine "complete" her stubbornly unfinished dream, and to prove to her that she is not going mad. (What else would this prove, then? That she was psychic? Reincarnated?) The connection with the Carlotta story is this: Carlotta was taken from the "mission settlement" where she grew up by her seducer, and Madeleine is obviously "remembering" childhood scenes in the mission.

11. He runs away, blacking out until he reaches his house.

12. Carlotta's.

13. Standing in front of the flower shop where Madeleine bought her posy.

14. Ernie's, the restaurant where Scottie first sees Madeleine, where he goes after her death, and where Scottie and Judy have their first meal together. Unfortunately, they don't make it back there that last night.

15. The necklace that Madeleine was wearing while dressing up as the Carlotta in the portrait at the Legion of Honor.

16. A nun rises from the shadows, causing her to step backward one too many times. This you will understand if you went to parochial school. "God have mercy," the nun says, the last words of the film.

17. Two, the policeman and Judy. The real Madeleine, you will recall, was already dead when Elster threw her over—he had broken her neck.

18. Both were innocent, beautiful women who were used by rich, cynical men for their own purposes and subsequently thrown away. The real Madeleine was also thrown away, in a more literal sense.

19. "By her own hand," Pop Liebel says. She was twenty-six, the same age, Elster says, as Madeleine.

20. Salina, Kansas. The address on her driver's license is 425 Maple Street.

21. Midge.

22. Hitchcock had a model of the stairway built on its side, then filmed it with the camera simultaneously zooming in and tracking back.

23. Vera Miles. The latest in Hitchcock's Pygmalion blondes, she bridled at his obsessive attention and control, so the story goes, and conveniently allowed herself to get pregnant.

NORTH BY NORTHWEST

1. Roger is an advertising executive.

2. He is trying to send a telegram to his mother.

3. Glen Cove, Long Island.

4. In George Kaplan's room at the Plaza. He lets the maid and the valet assume that he is Kaplan, but he doesn't identify himself as such until he calls down to the desk to ascertain where the immediately preceding call from Vandamm's thugs had come from. This time he stumbles over the name, but he gets increasingly more proficient.

5.   a. 3   d. 2
     b. 5   e. 4
     c. 1

6. In the hospital room after the phony shooting at the cafeteria. "A pint'll do," he says to the Professor.

7. The cafeteria scene, when he is forced into a bit of role-playing to save Eve's skin.

8. "Let's say he's a kind of . . . importer-exporter," the Professor says, and then, to the logical question "Of what?", "Oh, government secrets, perhaps."

9. In Kaplan's Plaza Hotel room.

10. Playing croquet, outside the window of Townsend's study.

11. After Roger escapes the crop duster and shows up at Kaplan's hotel in Chicago, the clerk tells him that Kaplan had checked out at 7:10 that morning. Given that Eve claimed to have gotten those nearly fatal directions from Kaplan in his hotel room at 9:10—two hours after he had checked out—Roger has cause to wonder about the woman's sincerity.

12. At the auction.

13. "What do I do with him in the morning?"

14. The highway on which Roger was to wait for Kaplan. (Anyone who mentions the additional words "Prairie Stop" may receive a whimsical number of points.)

15. The monogram on Thornhill's personalized matchbooks.

16. Nothing.

17. Indiana.

18. Leonard produces the gun filled with blanks with which Eve had allegedly shot Kaplan/Thornhill. Vandamm is not immediately grateful for the information.

19. She is after the statuette that is filled with microfilm.

20. Four.

21. Plaza Hotel, New York, Room 796; Ambassador East, Chicago; Sheraton-Johnson, Rapid City, South Dakota.

22. Five. Townsend, the thug Valarian and Leonard at Mount Rushmore, and *two* men in the crop duster. The Chicago *Sun Times* in Eve's hotel room tells us that there were two men in that plane, one of them the other original abductor (given the name Licht in the screenplay).

23. She is his sister. We hear this from Vandamm at the end as he is about to board the plane.

24. "Rather unsporting, don't you think . . . using real bullets?" Vandamm says to the Professor after Leonard is shot.

25. " . . .the expedient exaggeration." This is Roger's credo as dictated to his secretary at the beginning of the picture.

26. "I am but mad north-northwest: when the wind is southerly I know a hawk from a handsaw." (*Hamlet* II, ii)

PHOTO QUIZ III: DRAWING BLOOD ON THE RIGHT SIDE OF THE BRAIN

1. Mr. Van Meer, a Dutch diplomat, is *not* being assassinated in Amsterdam in *Foreign Correspondent*.

2. The spies shoot this double of Van Meer after having kidnapped the actual man. They do this to keep the police from looking for him, giving them time to worm the secret clause of the peace treaty from him.

3. She erases her name from this sketch in *Blackmail*. She leaves behind her gloves.

4. The artist prevails upon Alice to put on the dress so that she can pose for him. Unfortunately, the sight of Alice in the dress is too much for him to handle, and Alice is forced to knife him to death.

5. In the house of Dr. Alex Brulov, Constance's former teacher and psychoanalyst, in *Spellbound*.

6. The whiteness of Brulov's bathroom; the parallel lines on the bedspread similarly upset him.

7. In *Rope*, Rupert obviously has started to figure out what might have happened to David Kentley, and he has brought back the rope as the sign of his knowledge.

8. The first use was for David's murder. The second was the tying together of the first editions David's father was taking home.

9. The setting is Royal Albert Hall in *The Man Who Knew Too Much*.

10. Jill understands that an assassination is about to be attempted, much to her consternation.

MURDER THEME QUIZ

1. c *(Psycho)*

2. f *(Notorious)*

3. h *(Lifeboat)*

4. a *(Topaz)*

5. g *(The 39 Steps)*

6. b *(Blackmail)*

7. j *(Jamaica Inn)*

8. i *(The 39 Steps)*

9. d *(I Confess)*

10. e *(Marnie)*

11. Either Barbara Milligan or Brenda Blaney, courtesy Rob Rusk in *Frenzy*.

12. Gromek in *Torn Curtain*.

13. Miriam Haines in *Strangers on a Train*.

14. David Kentley in *Rope*.

15. Christine Clay in *Young and Innocent*.

16. Burned to death in their house by their adopted son Eddie in *Family Plot*.

17. Shot in the back by Dr. Murchison in *Spellbound*.

18. Hit by the proverbial blunt instrument by Otto Keller in *I Confess*.

19. Laid low by a poker by Jonathan Cooper in *Stage Fright*.

20. Also a poker, by Handell Fane in *Murder!*

21. Tony, the defense plant worker in *Saboteur*.

22. The theater patron in *Saboteur*, the merry-go-round operator in *Strangers on a Train*, the hotel cook in *I Confess*, or, it may be argued, any of the victims of the saboteurs' bombs in *Sabotage* and *Saboteur*.

23. Louis Bernard, of course, in the 1934 and 1956 versions of *The Man Who Knew Too Much*.

QUOTES QUIZ II

1. *Murder!*, Diana Baring (Nora Baring).

2. *To Catch a Thief*, Frances Stevens (Grace Kelly).

3. *Frenzy*, Bob Rusk (Barry Foster).

4. *The Lodger*, Joe Betts (Malcolm Keen).

5. *Shadow of a Doubt*, Charlie Newton (Teresa Wright).

6. *Marnie*, Marnie Edgar (Tippi Hedren).

7. *Notorious*, Alex Sebastian (Claude Rains).

8. *The Wrong Man*, the real thief, name of Daniel (Richard Robbins).

9. *Rebecca*, Mrs. van Hopper (Florence Bates) and Maxim de Winter (Laurence Olivier).

10. *Strangers on a Train*, Barbara Morton (Patricia Hitchcock).

11. *Under Capricorn*, Charles Adare (Michael Wilding).

12. *Suspicion*, Mrs. Newsham (Isabel Jeans).

13. *North by Northwest*, Clara Thornhill (Jessie Royce Landis).

14. *Secret Agent*, Richard Ashenden (John Gielgud).

15. *The Trouble With Harry*, Jennifer Rogers (Shirley MacLaine).

16. *Foreign Correspondent*, Johnny Jones/Huntley Haverstock (Joel Mc-Crea).

17. *North by Northwest*, Leonard (Martin Landau).

18. *Spellbound*, "Dr. Edwardes," alias John Brown, alias John Ballantine (Gregory Peck).

19. *Rope*, Brandon Shaw (John Dall).

20. *Torn Curtain*, Sarah Sherman (Julie Andrews).

PSYCHO

1. Phoenix. Friday, December 11, 2:43 P.M.

2. Forty thousand dollars. Marion spends seven hundred dollars on the car at California Charlie's.

3. Marion hides the remainder of the money in a copy of the Los Angeles

Times, which Norman tosses into the trunk of her car before sinking it into the swamp. So, "swamp" is the answer for the more taciturn; that is Dr. Richman's answer as well. (In deference to the more literal-minded, it must be noted that the very last shot of *Psycho* shows a car being towed out of the swamp. Thus, it may be justly hypothesized that if the car was Marion's, the money was recovered.)

4. Her mother.

5. His father, who died and left him debts, and his ex-wife, who collects alimony while she's . . . "living on the other side of the world some-where!" This angry outburst is triggered by Marion's desire for respect-ability, something else that requires a lot of sweating-out as far as Sam is concerned.

6. Five years old.

7. "Mother" is concerned that Norman will seduce the woman. "As if people don't desire strangers," she says sarcastically, apparently afraid she'll miss out on something. She doesn't, in the end.

8. Suicide. Sheriff Chambers says, "Mrs. Bates poisoned this guy she was involved with when she found out he was married—then took a helpin' of the stuff herself. Strychnine. Ugly way to die." "Norman found them together . . . *in bed!*" Mrs. Chambers thoughtfully amplifies.

9. When Norman carries her down to the fruit cellar after Arbogast's murder.

10. Mrs. Bates's lover talked her into it. "He could've talked her into anything."

11. The highway that the motel was originally built to service has been moved.

12. Marie Samuels of Los Angeles.

13. Cabin 1—in case she needs anything, Norman says. There are twelve cabins in all. "Twelve cabins, twelve vacancies."

14. Taxidermy is Norman's hobby. Mrs. Bates serves as his most accom-plished subject.

15. That Mother be put away.

16. A painting, apparently of a rape. Spoto reports that the scene is of the story of Susanna and the Elders, told in the book of Daniel, Chapter 13 of the Catholic Bible, in which the virtuous Susanna is overtaken in her bath by two lascivious elders of the town.

17. "Mother! Oh, God, Mother. Blood!" Norman says.

18. A painless insecticide. "I say, insect or man, death should always be painless," the customer says.

19. After Arbogast's murder, he is afraid that more cops will come snooping around and discover her.

20. The color of the dress Mrs. Bates was buried in, or almost buried in. Mrs. Chambers remembers it fondly; she helped Norman pick it out.

21. b. The indentation of a human form.

22. e. The "Eroica."

23. b. A hardware store, dubbed Sam Loomis Hardware, appropriately.

24. Cassidy, the man with the $40,000 in Phoenix. Or at least Marion imagines him saying this as she drives in the rain to the Bates Motel.

25. Nine. The movie starts on Friday. Marion is killed on Saturday night. A week passes before Lila visits Sam—he dates the letter he is writing to Marion on the Sam Loomis Hardware stationery "Saturday"—and Arbogast mentions to Norman that Marion has been gone "about a week." Sam and Lila get the sheriff out of bed that night and talk to him as he leaves church the next day: Sunday. Turning down a home-cooked meal, they then go to the Bates Motel and get to the root of the problem. Nine days.

26. The shower scene. Perkins was in New York during the week the scene was filmed, preparing for a play.

27. Chocolate sauce.

28. Florrie.

29. A torn piece of paper on which she has subtracted $700 from $40,000. Some powerful figuring. Lila later finds part of the paper that did not flush and notices that some number had been added to or subtracted from $40,000. "That proves that Marion was here," she says. "It would be too wild a coincidence!"

THE BIRDS

1. Melanie has come for a mynah bird, Mitch for lovebirds.

2. Mitch, an attorney, had seen Melanie in court when one of her "little practical jokes" had broken a plate-glass window. At least that's what Mitch says.

3. Melanie had a reporter from her father's paper track down Mitch's license plate at the Division of Motor Vehicles. Knowledge of the license plate number—wJH 003—is certainly worth an extra point.

4. The men at the general store in Bodega Bay directed her to Annie Hayworth's house—Annie knew it, being the schoolteacher and Cathy's teacher (and apparently everyone else's).

5. d, g, h, b, a, f, e, c.

6. a. crows   e. gulls and crows
    b. sparrows   f. gulls
    c. gulls and crows   g. a gull
    d. a gull   h. gulls

7. "Oh, I see," they both say, when it becomes clear whose benefit the lovebirds have really been brought for.

8. Melanie's father is part-owner of the *Daily News* in San Francisco. Melanie's mother ran off with "some hotel man from the East" when Melanie was eleven; she has not heard from her since.

9. Frank Brenner has been dead four years. Lydia speaks of him as having the ability to enter into their children's world, something she is unable to do. Annie spoke earlier of Lydia's inability to give Mitch the love that he needs.

10. Seems the papers reported Melanie jumped naked into a fountain in Rome. Melanie claims she was pushed in, with all her clothes on.

11. About four years, since around the time of Frank Brenner's death. She moved to Bodega Bay after she knew it was hopeless with old Mitch, just to be near him. (She says that!)

12. Working in her garden. An earth mother.

13. Mondays and Wednesdays she works at Traveler's Aid at the airport; on Tuesdays she takes a general semantics course at Berkeley; on Thursday she participates in a "meeting and lunch" that puts a Korean boy through school.

14. She is curious why neither her chickens nor *his* chickens are eating. Fred Brinkmeyer, the feed salesman, told her about Dan Fawcett's chickens.

15. The Tides Restaurant.

16. The hysterical mother proposes that Melanie is a witch and is the cause of the birds' attacks. Melanie slaps her, appropriately enough.

17. "It's the end of the world," he says at the slightest provocation, quoting from the book of Ezekiel.

18. The bellicose businessman (this is beginning to look like a demographic target group for conservative direct mail) proposes that all birds be wiped off the face of the earth with guns, the dirty animals. The or-

nithologist points out that this would be even more impossible than slapping all the hysterical mothers in the world to their senses. Soon afterward the businessman is engulfed in flames, along with his car, when he attempts to douse his match in a nearby puddle of gasoline.

19. The story begins on Friday morning and ends on Tuesday morning.

20. Annie and Cathy were inside Annie's house, but came out when they heard the explosion of the gas station, curious as to the cause. Annie was immediately set upon by unfriendly crows.

21. The Trautonium, a machine designed by one Friedrich Trautwein. The electronic soundtrack for *The Birds* was created by Remi Gassman and Oskar Sala, overseen by Bernard Herrmann.

22. Cathy is eleven, the same age Melanie was when her mother left.

MARNIE

1. Mark is a publisher. Strutt is his tax assessor, and a victim of Marnie's.

2. Lil is Mark's sister-in-law, the sister of his dead wife, who continued living at the Rutland house even after her sister had died.

3. Red gladioli.

4. A man named Ward, a former victim, happens upon them at the racetrack and remembers Marnie as Peggy Nicholson.

5. She invites Strutt, the last victim of Marnie's kleptomania, to the party at the Rutlands'. Strutt is restrained from revenge only by Mark's blackmail (of a sort).

6. A pre-Columbian vase, belonging to his first wife Stella, is broken during the storm in Mark's office. Mark's reaction is, "We've all got to go sometime."

7. "There—there now."

8. She is lame—and walks with a cane—as a result of the sailor falling on her leg after Marnie killed him. It is this leg that Marnie invariably aggravates in her pleas for affection.

9. Jessie, a girl from her neighborhood.

10. Forio.

11. Evan Hunter. According to Spoto, Hunter and Hitchcock had a falling-out over the rape scene, which Hunter thought very ill-advised. Hitchcock, unused to being contradicted, preferred not to deal with Hunter

any longer. Jay Presson Allen subsequently took over the screenwriting.

12. Grace Kelly, who evidently was ready to accept before a dispute between de Gaulle and Ranier caused her to pull out of the project.

TORN CURTAIN

1. An antimissile missile. Gamma 5 was the name of the American project. (How do you like this irony: Paul Newman goes to all this trouble to get the formula and then Congress kills the ABM. Ingrates.)

2. The International Congress of Physics is to convene in Copenhagen.

3. "Your book is ready—Elmo Book Shop."

4. π is the name of the resistance organization (3.14 is an insufficient answer). Michael gets this information from the book he picks up at the Elmo Book Shop: "See p. 107," a note on the first page says, leading us to the symbol which is circled for easy recognition.

5. Gromek lived once upon a time in New York—Eighty-eighth and Eighth, he says (possibly for the alliteration, since no such corner exists). It finally becomes clear Gromek will have to be killed when he indicates he is familiar with the π sign Michael has scrawled in the dirt and then begins to call for reinforcements.

6. He tells her he is going to Stockholm, to speak to the Swedish Defense Department.

7. She is sitting next to Sarah on the plane to East Berlin. She calls the cops twice, first in the theater and again the following day when she suspects that Michael and Sarah are in the costume baskets at sea.

8. Koska is the doctor at Leipzig University; Albert is the contact at the Friedrichstrasse Post Office in Berlin; Hugo is the chap with the red hair (which is not his own) who smuggles them into the costume baskets backstage at the theater; Herr Jacobi is the father figure aboard the π bus to Berlin. The busted operation is at the travel agency that Jacobi directs the couple to; they meet their contact across the street.

9. a. The police roadblock.
   b. The holdup.
   c. The hysterical woman is let off.
   d. They are forced to pick up a real passenger, the old woman.
   e. The hysterical woman's name is Fräulein Mann.

10. Lindt's has worked, Michael's has not.

11. Czechoslovakia.

12. The obvious one: Michael yells fire in a crowded theater. The somewhat less obvious one: Herr Jacobi leans forward to light a cigarette for another π passenger, thereby shielding the couple from the view of the soldiers who are searching the π bus.

13. Bernard Herrmann had done his usual work for Hitchcock's latest movie (which he had been doing faithfully since *The Trouble With Harry* a decade before), but Hitchcock angrily rejected it, purportedly under pressure from Universal, which wanted a more commercial, Mancini-like singable score.

TOPAZ

1. Topaz is the code name for a Communist spy group in the highest levels of French security.

2. Copenhagen, Washington, New York, Cuba and Paris.

3. The Cuban Missile Crisis of 1962.

4. The CIA asks Dévereaux to obtain a copy of a treaty between Cuba and the USSR, which is currently in the possession of the Cuban Rico Parra. Prior to his appearance at the United Nations, Parra is holing up at the Theresa Hotel in Harlem. (Mention of the hotel is certainly worth 2 points.)

5. Uribe is Rico Parra's secretary. Nordstrom hears that he hates Americans because he lost a son at the Bay of Pigs.

6. She is the widow of a hero of the revolution, and she is Parra's mistress, at least while Dévereaux is not in town.

7. In the endpapers of the book Juanita gives him. He thinks it is in the typewriter and the head of his shaver, but it isn't. (Juanita has probably lied to him about where it is so he can't look guiltily at the book while they're searching him at the airport.)

8. Kusenov was deputy chief of the KGB. Jarré is an economist with NATO.

9. a. Columbine is the Soviet code name for the head of Topaz, who turns out to be Jacques Granville.
   b. Den Permanente is the store in Copenhagen where the Kusenovs are spirited away by the CIA into the West.

10. Much significance, are you kidding? It is Columbine's phone number; Jarré dials it in François Picard's presence and we are led to the traitor,

Jacques Granville. Nicole Dévereaux knows its significance, because she uses it—she is sleeping with the man.

11. The first was a duel between Dévereaux and Granville, in which the latter was killed by a sniper (to ensure his silence? We can't say—we are getting all this third-hand). The second involved Granville's successful flight to the Communist bloc. Truffaut reports that both endings were laughed at by preview audiences.

12. Michel Piccoli, who played Granville, was no longer available—this was long after production had stopped—and the only footage of a man entering the Granville house was of Henri Jarré, who walked with a very noticeable limp and a cane. So the film was concluded with the briefest of shots of a man entering the house (the last few centimeters of Jarré's body, after the telltale cane had entered), a frozen frame and a gunshot. Very awkward.

FRENZY

1. Covent Garden. Hitchcock's father was a greengrocer in the same area. Today Covent Garden is a tourist trap, full of little shops.

2. Inspector Oxford and Sir George, the politician who is giving the speech at the beginning of the film. "I say, is that my club tie?" Sir George wonders.

3. One—the Salvation Army hostel. Two—the Coburg Hotel. Three— the Porters' apartment. Four—jail. The Cupid Room is the Coburg's specialty room.

4. Blaney: the face powder from Brenda's handbag, traces of which were on the money he used to pay for the Coburg Hotel room. Rusk: dust from the potatoes he wrestled with while retrieving his tiepin from Babs's body. The dust was also present on a clothes brush that Rusk used at the café. (Presumably the owner had not used the brush since.)

5. "You're my kind of girl."

6. Extreme cruelty. "Mentally and physically," Hattie Porter adds, helpfully.

7. Brenda Blaney's lunch.

8, The Continental School of Gourmet Cooking.

9. Johnny Porter has convinced Blaney and Babs to go to Paris with him, where he is operating an English-style pub.

10. The RAF. Blaney and Johnny were at Suez together.

11. Beekeeping.

12. Coming Up.

13. A margarita. Quite an exotic drink, apparently, in Hitchcock's England.

14. Henry Mancini. Ironically, the same thing happened to Mancini (who was more accustomed to those "pop" scores Hollywood is so fond of) as to Bernard Herrmann. Mancini evidently wrote a score he thought sounded like Herrmann and Hitchcock rejected it. Ron Goodwin eventually did the music.

FAMILY PLOT

1. It's empty. Even though Harry and Sadie Shoebridge, buried in the same grave, died the same year as Eddie, Eddie's headstone is much newer.

2. Her sister, Harriet. Harriet, now departed, is still sore because Julia forced her to give up her illegitimate son in order to avoid a scandal more than forty years before.

3. Adamson thinks Blanche and George are wise to the kidnappings he has been pulling off with his consort, Frances. Adamson is eager not to be identified as Eddie Shoebridge because Eddie Shoebridge had his house set on fire and his (adoptive) parents burned to death some years earlier.

4. From Mrs. Hannigan, the daughter of the Rainbirds' chauffeur in the days of the bastard birth.

5. From the Registrar of Births and Deaths, and from the application for a death certificate (denied for lack of evidence) that Maloney had been careless enough to leave extant.

6. From Mrs. Maloney, who spills the beans to George at her husband's funeral, and afterward takes out her frustration at the absent troublemaker by kicking over his damnable Eddie Shoebridge headstone.

7. Fifteen. The Shoebridges died in 1950; the application is dated 1965.

8. He and Frances spot George at Bishop Wood's kidnapping, and are finally sure that the couple are onto them. George, of course, is there for a completely different reason.

9. Mrs. Rainbird remembers that at the time of the adoption there was one person—the local parson, now Bishop Wood—who promised always to be aware of the Rainbird child's fortunes. There is no evidence that he was able to; Adamson seems to have kidnapped him purely for sentimental reasons.

10. Henry.

11. Michael O'Keefe.

12. Abe and Mabel's.

13. Roy Thinnes, reportedly the only actor that Hitchcock ever fired.

14. Variously, *Deceit* or *Deception*.

PHOTO QUIZ IV: THE BOSOM OF JUSTICE AND OTHER INTERESTING PLACES

1. In the Statue of Liberty in *Saboteur*.

2. Fry falls to his death.

3. George Lumley in *Family Plot*.

4. George finds out an application for a death certificate for the man he is investigating, Eddie Shoebridge, was filed some time ago, but years after Shoebridge had supposedly died. The request was denied for lack of a body.

5. Bruno has dropped Guy's cigarette lighter in *Strangers on a Train*.

6. The lighter is Bruno's device for framing Guy, which he is planning to deposit at the scene of his own crime.

7. Barbara Milligan's in *Frenzy*.

8. Bob Rusk has put them there, framing his old friend, Dick.

9. His name is Harry Warp of *The Trouble With Harry*. He is dead.

10. First, a tramp steals them. Calvin Wiggs, Deputy Sheriff, takes them from the tramp, and Captain Wiles pinches them from Wiggs's truck.

THE WRONG MAN THEME QUIZ

1. Michael Logan, Otto Keller, *I Confess*.

2. Barry Kane, Fry, *Saboteur*.

3. Richard Hannay, Professor Jordan (at least by implication), *The 39 Steps*.

4. John Robie, Danielle Foussard, *To Catch a Thief*.

5. Richard Blaney, Bob Rusk, *Frenzy*.

6. George Kaplan.

7. First of all, of being a U.S. government agent by Vandamm and company, and secondly, of killing Lester Townsend by the police.

8. Robbing his insurance company, Associated Life.

9. Trying to hold up a grocery store. He is foiled by the knife-wielding proprietress.

10. The jewel heists are being performed in his old style, with clues left that pointedly indicate the Cat as the perpetrator.

11. Danielle is the daughter of a former accomplice and fellow member of the French Underground.

12. Logan, a priest, took Keller's confession in his formal office, in the confessional, and cannot as a matter of professional ethics reveal such a secret to the police.

13. His former lover, Ruth Grandfort, was being blackmailed by the murdered man, Villette.

14. A defense plant.

15. He read Fry's name on an envelope the man dropped a few minutes previous to the fire. Fry snatches it back with a scowl.

16. A black bag, which the Avenger and the Lodger both carry with them on Tuesdays. In the Lodger's bag are a gun, a bunch of newspaper clippings of Avenger crimes, and a map of recent Avenger strikes.

17. The hand of the fair Daisy, who is proving uncooperative and has an eye for the Lodger. "When I've put a rope around the Avenger's neck, I'll put a ring around Daisy's finger," Joe says.

18. Murdering Miss Annabella Smith.

19. An irritating facial tic.

20. The belt from Robert's raincoat, which, it turns out, was the murder weapon.

21. Brenda Blaney, his ex-wife, and Barbara Milligan, his girlfriend.

22. Bob Rusk, the murderer.

23. A hat. In *The Wrong Man* Manny is picked out of a lineup mainly because the hat makes him look similar to the thief. In *The Lodger*, our protagonist wears the same hat and face-concealing scarf as the Avenger.

24. Robert Tisdall, Michael Logan, John Robie, Roger Thornhill.

25. In *Spellbound*, John Ballantine, aka John Brown, believes, at least for a time, that he actually murdered Dr. Edwardes and took his place.

26. The villain, Philip Vandamm, if you recall, assumed the name Lester Townsend—even commandeered his house and dispensed his liquor liberally—the day before Lester Townsend was murdered at his order.

27. They are both planning to kill the real killer, the Lodger avenging the death of his sister, Richard Blaney avenging his own betrayal.

28. Mr. Caypor, who is killed by the General and Ashenden in *Secret Agent*.

29. Jonathan Cooper in *Stage Fright*. We are led to believe through most of the film that Jonathan is innocent of killing Charlotte Inwood's husband. It turns out that he is actually guilty.

THE MACGUFFIN THEME QUIZ

1. e   6. a
2. g   7. h
3. i   8. j
4. b   9. d
5. c   10. f

11. Both the little old man, in *Foreign Correspondent*, and the little old lady, in *The Lady Vanishes*—Mr. Van Meer and Miss Froy, respectively—carry the secret clauses to peace treaties. Miss Froy's clause is encoded in a tune.

12. Angus MacPhail.

THE END-OF-THE-BOOK QUIZ

1. *Blackmail, North by Northwest, Rear Window, Saboteur, Shadow of a Doubt, The Man Who Knew Too Much* (both versions), *Murder!, Jamaica Inn, Vertigo*, and, arguably, *To Catch a Thief* and *The Lodger*.

2. *North by Northwest:* Leonard picks up the matchbook Roger is using to signal Eve. *Spellbound:* Dr. Murchison picks up a note from John Brown/Ballantine and thoughtfully hands it to Constance.

3. Carlotta Valdes, *Vertigo;* Rebecca; Harry Warp, *The Trouble With Harry;* Mr. Brenner, *The Birds;* Major Paradine, *The Paradine Case;* General McLaidlaw, *Suspicion*.

4. Uncle Charlie, *Shadow of a Doubt*. Tony Wendice, *Dial M for Murder*.

5. The finger: *Dial M for Murder*, dialing M on the big dial. The hand:

Spellbound, Dr. Murchison's suicide. The glasses of brandy: *The Lady Vanishes,* the drugged drinks sitting next to Dr. Hartz, waiting for our heroes.

6. Jonathan Cooper, *Stage Fright;* Otto Keller, *I Confess;* Mr. Memory, *The 39 Steps;* Rien, the assassin, *The Man Who Knew Too Much* (1956); man in audience, *Saboteur.*

7. Handell Fane, *Murder!;* Bruno Anthony, *Strangers on a Train.*

8. Brandon Shaw, *Rope;* Tony Wendice, *Dial M for Murder.*

9. Cold cream: Mrs. van Hopper, *Rebecca;* Eggs: Jessie Stevens, *To Catch a Thief.*

10. Jonathan Cooper, *Stage Fright;* Bob Rusk, *Frenzy.*

11. a. *Psycho.*
     b. *The Wrong Man.*
     c. *Under Capricorn.*

12. a. *Rebecca.*   g. *Spellbound.*
     b. *Strangers on a Train.*   h. *Marnie.*
     c. *The Man Who Knew Too Much* (1956).   i. *Psycho.*
     d. *Suspicion.*   j. *Shadow of a Doubt.*
     e. *Vertigo.*   k. *Family Plot.*
     f. *The Birds.*

13. a. *Foreign Correspondent.*   d. *Saboteur.*
     b. *Topaz.*   e. *Torn Curtain.*
     c. *North by Northwest.*

14. a. Otto Keller.   c. Charles Tobin.
     b. Alma Keller.   d. Mrs. Van Sutton.

15. *Bon Voyage* and *Aventure Malgache.*

16. *Foreign Correspondent.*